LIFESTORY ENCOUNTERS

DANIEL R. SÁNCHEZ
J.O. TERRY

Church Starting Network

LifeStory Encounters
Copyright 2009 Daniel R. Sánchez and J. O. Terry

Address requests for information to:
Church Starting Network
3515 Sycamore School Road
Fort Worth, Texas 76133

www.ChurchStarting.net
smith_ebbie@yahoo.com

Library of Congress Cataloging-in-Publication Data

Daniel R. Sánchez and J. O. Terry
LifeStory Encounters

ISBN13   978-0-9820875-6-5
ISBN10   0-9820875-6-x

All rights reserved. No part of this publication may be reproduced, stored in a retrieval system, or transmitted in any form by any means—electronic, mechanical, photocopy, recording, or any other—except for brief quotations in printed reviews, without the prior permission of the publisher.

Printed in Canada

OTHER PUBLICATIONS

J.O Terry, *Basic Bible Storying*. Ft. Worth, Texas: Church Starting Network, 2006.

Daniel R. Sánchez, J.O. Terry, LaNette Thompson, *Bible Storying for Church Planting*. Ft. Worth, Texas: Church Starting Network, 2008.

J.O. Terry, *Bible Storying Handbook: For Short-Term Church Mission Teams and Mission Volunteers*. Ft. Worth, Texas: Church Starting Network, 2008.

J.O. Terry, *Guía Para La Narrativa Bíblica* (Synopsis of the Bible Storying Handbook, translated into Spanish by Keith Stamps). Ft. Worth, Texas: Church Starting Network, 2008.

J.O. Terry, *Hope Stories from the Bible*. Ft. Worth, Texas: Church Starting Network, 2008.

Daniel R. Sánchez, *Sharing the Good News with Roman Catholic Friends*. Ft. Worth, Texas: Church Starting Network, 2004.

Daniel R. Sánchez, *Gospel in the Rosary*. Ft. Worth, Texas: Church Starting Network, 2004

All of these can be obtained through the Church Starting Network
www.ChurchStarting.net
3515 Sycamore School Road, Fort Worth, Texas 76133

ACKNOWLEDGEMENTS

We want to express our profound appreciation to some very special people who directly or indirectly contributed to the publication of this book. Through his excellent booklet, *LifeStory Conversations*, Dr. Roy W. Fairchild inspired us and enabled us to focus more clearly on the importance of listening to a person's Life Story, sharing our Life Story, and going to His (Christ's) story.

We are also indebted to a large number of people whose life stories we included in our book. Without their knowing it, their life stories provided excellent examples of the manner in which personal experiences can become bridges leading to the sharing of His Story.

The authors wish to inform readers that in some places illustrations or examples of stories will be interjected into the text. The authors will indicate these sections by the use of subtitles such as "**Example: A Successful Musician.**" The forms of these subtitles indicate they are examples and do not follow the usual organization of the chapters.

CONTENTS

Chapter   **Page**

Introduction vi

1. Preparing to Tell the Story 1
   Daniel R. Sánchez
2. Inspiring Lifestory Encounters 27
   Daniel R. Sánchez
3. Personal Lifestories 51
   J.O. Terry
4. The Value of Utilizing Life Stories 71
   J.O. Terry
5. Bridging Bible Stories 107
   J.O. Terry and Daniel R. Sánchez

Conclusion 131

Endnotes 135

INTRODUCTION

The Bible records inspiring examples of the manner in which various communicators used stories to set the stage for the proclamation of divine truth. Both the stories these witnesses used and the methods of using stories help proclaimers today employ storying as a means to share the Good News.

When the prophet, Nathan, faced the task of communicating God's message to King David, he initiated the conversation with a story (2 Samuel 12). He told of a wealthy man who possessed many sheep. In order to feed a guest who arrived unexpectedly, the wealthy man killed the only sheep that a poor man possessed. In an addition to the story, the prophet indicated that the sheep was a beloved family pet.

Incensed by the actions in the story, King David declared: "That man deserves to die." To which pronouncement, Nathan responded: "You are that man." Nathan then communicated God's message to King David.

When facing the need to communicate God's love to the Pharisees who were criticizing him for "eating with sinners," Jesus told the story of the "Prodigal Son" (Luke 15). Those who heard this story in the days of Jesus and who hear it today understand that the father in the story represented the Heavenly Father, that the Prodigal Son represented repentant sinners, and that the Older Son represented the self-righteous Pharisees. This story continues to be a marvelous instrument to assure people of God's love, forgiveness, and desire to fellowship with them. The story also continues to show the evil of self-righteousness that overlooks the needs of others.

The Apostle Paul was a prisoner in chains when he faced the awesome task of communicating the Gospel message to King Agripa. Paul began with his own story (Acts 26:1-22). He recounted the way he was brought up as a highly trained Jewish lad and later became a devout Pharisee. He told of the way that in his zeal he persecuted Christians, throwing them in jail. He shared the miraculous encounter he had with Jesus on the road to Damascus, the way in which Jesus totally changed his life, and the new mission Jesus had given to communicate the message of salvation.

After telling his own story, Paul moved on to tell His (Jesus') story (vv. 22, 23). This story was the account of the fulfillment of the prophecies concerning the death and resurrection of Jesus. Paul then gave Agripa an opportunity to place his faith in Jesus (vv. 27-29).

Stories have a way of capturing the attention of people, cutting through layers of preconceived notions, and engaging the listeners intellectually, emotionally, and spiritually. There is a sense in which a story is like a "Trojan horse." Once it enters the heart it begins to work from within to communicate divine truths that resonate with the soul of the individual.

Certainly, stories have marvelous potential for communicating the message of salvation. One of the most difficult tasks, however, is that of knowing when and where to tell a story in such a way that people will listen attentively and receptively. There are times when hearing **their story** can open the way for you to tell them **your story** and prepare the way for you to share **His Story**.

The purpose of this book is:

- to inform our readers about the exciting manner in which LifeStory Encounters can be used as a very effective evangelistic instrument
- to guide our readers in the review of their own personal story and
- to enable them to share His (Christ's) story with wisdom, confidence, and enthusiasm.

It is also our hope that *LifeStory Encounters* will open the door for many people to become involved in the long-term evangelistic, discipleship, and church-planting group approaches such as Chronological Bible Storying. Our prayer is that the other books we have written, *Basic Bible Storying,*[1] *Bible Storying for Church Planting,*[2] *Bible Storying Handbook: For Short-Term Church Mission Teams and Mission Volunteers,*[3] *Hope Stories from The Bible,*[4] and *Guía Para La Narrativa Biblica*[5] will be good resources for those seeking to impact entire communities with the gospel message.

The expression "*LifeStory*" has been used deliberately as a single word to speak about our lives and our stories which really cannot be separated. Stories speak of a life and its adventures and encounters. Life is itself a story that we think of as beginning the day of our birth and ending the day of our death.

Circumstances that affect our lives, however, often begin long before birth and have consequences and influences on many others even following our death. The authors of this book pray that our efforts will serve to raise your awareness of the value of your LifeStory and how to use it for the glory of God and for ministering to those who find solace in trusting their LifeStories to you.

Your LifeStory is a bridge from someone's LifeStory to God's Story. Your LifeStory is a supplement to the Bible stories by providing a relational conversational bridge with empathy and possibly supplying an illustration or application of God's Story at work in your life.

In our effort to accomplish the objective of *LifeStory Encounters*, J.O. Terry and Daniel R. Sánchez will not only share vital concepts about storying through life experience but will supply a significant number of inspiring and instructive examples of how this ministry is being done.

CHAPTER 1

PREPARING TO TELL THE STORY

Daniel R. Sánchez

In his informative and inspiring booklet, *LifeStory Conversations*, Roy W. Fairchild offers helpful suggestions on how we can share the Good News of salvation in a way that takes into account our life pilgrimage as well as that of the person with whom we are conversing.[6] He asserts that a LifeStory conversation is a way of listening to a person's story, sharing our story, and focusing on The Story (the story of Jesus). In his words it is "the art of sharing personal stories and searching together for the relationship between our stories and The Story."[7]

Our Story and "The Story"

The starting point in this process of witnessing is coming to a better understanding of our own story and initially sharing it with those who are closest to us spiritually. This involves doing a life review, connecting the dots, clarifying our values, and linking our story with Christ's story.[8] The storying method makes much of using one's own story as a foundation for communication.

Analyzing your LifeStory

In order to do a life review, we need begin by analyzing our past. As we reflect on where we have been, we are better able to understand where we are now, and where we are going. Fairchild believes that "unless we survey accomplishments, regrets, high and low points of past experiences, the celebrations, and the wilderness experiences, we cannot begin to perceive how God has been working in our story."[9] When we come to a realization of the manner in which God has been working in our lives through the various experiences we have had, we are in a better position to understand our story and to know how to share it with others.

Connecting the Dots

The search for inner meaning in our own life experiences helps us to find divinely ordered patterns that provide evidence of God's mighty work in our lives. Fairchild explains:

> It is possible that a life which has been viewed as a simple series of individual happenings - as fragments, splinters, and broken-off pieces - can be joined together in conversation by a thread of meaning that runs through them all... Were it not for Zaccheus' "life review" in his home with Jesus and his disclosure of his extortion of his fellow Jews through surplus taxation (Luke 10:1-10), how could this little man have decided to make restitution to those he had cheated and begin a new story?[10]

LifeStory conversations involve the search for the inner meanings of outward events in our lives. The crucial matter is not what individual experiences we have had but how we have seen the hand of God in and through them. Seeing the inner meanings of these experiences enables us to understand our Christian pilgrimage and helps us to share it with others.

Clarifying Your Values

As a believer reviews his/her LifeStory, the witness often comes to a clarification of his/her values. What were our values in the past? How have these experiences (especially our experience with Christ) changed our values? What is it that actually counts in my life today (money, power, possessions, reputation, security, love, pleasure, faithfulness, health, or something else)?

I was sitting in the hospital with our desperately ill baby daughter when the phone rang. My wife, on the way to the hospital, had been involved in a car accident. She was crying when she told me that "our new car was totally ruined." I then asked her, "Are you and Danny (our six year old son) ok?" When she said that they were, I thanked God and breathed a deep sigh of relief. The last thing on my mind was the condition of our car. Our baby was fighting for her life and nothing else was important. There are times when the values of life, love, health, family, and our relationship with the Lord overshadow any other thing that might be important to us. Actually, should not this be so always?

A seminary professor, whose baby had been born with a severe birth defect, held out the keys to his brand new home and told his students, "I would gladly give these up if only my little guy could walk." What are the values that are closest to our hearts? Clarifying these can help us to have meaningful conversations with people about the values that really count. Going from these to spiritual values can be accomplished in a very natural and meaningful way.

Going From Your Story To The Story

Going from *our* story to *The* Story involves discerning the activity of God in the concrete events of our lives. Upon meeting his brothers in Egypt, Joseph reflected on their cruelty, his hardships, his exile, and his subsequent position of influence and power in the new land. He told his brothers: "*You meant it for evil, but God meant it for good*" (Genesis 50:20)[11]

Looking back at our lives, what have been the crucial hinge points in which God's presence and guidance have made a difference? It is helpful for us to reflect on the experiences we have had (positive, negative, joyous, painful, victorious, and disappointing) and to seek to discern the hand of God through it all. How has God delivered us from the painful and hurtful experiences? How have we seen the hand of God in the victories and affirmations that have been ours?

Looking back at our story, what evidences can we see that God was guiding our lives so that His purpose could be accomplished in us? Fairchild reminds us that: "When a person senses God is a companion in the journey of life, his/her story begins to merge with The Story."[12]

Sharing Your Story with Fellow Christians

After we have done our life review, searched for meaning, clarified our values, and linked our story with *The* Story, it is essential to share our story with key fellow Christians. We can help one another to sharpen the way in which we share our stories, to ensure that we refrain from using a lot of "religious vocabulary," and to make sure that our story is brief and focused. The "themes" that we will discuss below will be helpful in designing the best way to share our story.

The process will begin with considering principles of how we should listen carefully to their stories.

Listening to Their Story

Few practices are more important in relationships than the simple matter of listening to others. Christian witnesses should develop the skill of carefully listening to others. A first principle of LifeStory methods relates squarely to the matter of simply listening to people.

Christians often experience great anxiety about what they are going to say in witnessing situations. They seem to forget that Jesus often dialogued with people. John 3 records Jesus' conversation with Nicodemus. The Lord began by listening to what Nicodemus had to say about his desire to meet Jesus. He made some statements and then listened to Nicodemus' questions. Jesus' response prompted even more questions from Nicodemus. The conversation was a dialog and not a monolog.

The same principle was true of Jesus' conversation with the Samaritan woman. From these and other examples, we understand that the importance for us to know that often the first step is to listen to what people have to say. This procedure will provide us a clue as to the best way to share the story of Jesus with them.

Many times as we engage people in conversation, they will mention an experience that they have had or are having that falls under the broad categories of the four themes discussed bellow. The insight into their experience we gain from listening to their stories will often open the door for us to share with them an experience related to a similar theme (a slice of life) and explain how our personal faith in Christ made the greatest difference in the world.

LifeStory Themes

When people talk about their stories, they will often refer to a wide variety of experiences. These experiences, however, can generally be grouped into four major themes that Fairchild suggests.[13] The themes are:

- joys and achievements,
- life-changing events,
- sorrows and difficulties,
- changes and challenges.

I will briefly explain these themes and then share experiences that I have had while conversing with people about their LifeStories.

Joys and Achievements

Most of the joys discussed in LifeStory conversations center around areas of love and friendship, work achievements, service to others, and the expression of our own creative individuality. Many times after people have experienced a high point in their lives, they are ready and willing to talk about it. The event that is foremost in the person's mind could be a personal accomplishment, a victory of one of their family members, an addition to the family, or even a "win" obtained by their favorite sports teams.[14]

Example: A Successful Musician

A number of years ago I was on board an airplane going from Atlanta to New York City. Sitting next to me was a young man who appeared to be friendly but was not overly talkative at the time. After we chatted briefly, I asked him: "What has been the greatest experience of your life?"

He thought for a moment and said: "The greatest experience of my life was when I played at Carnegie Hall."

"Wow," I said, "that sounds interesting. Tell me about it."

He explained: "I'm a classical guitarist. After many years of practicing and playing in many places I came to the point when my teacher felt that I was ready to play at Carnegie."

"What was it like?" I asked. "Were you very nervous?"

"Oh yes," he said, "I was quite nervous, especially knowing that there were many music critics in the audience."

He added: "As soon as I started playing, I was able to concentrate on my music. It helped a lot that the people applauded enthusiastically on my first piece. From then on, it was sheer enjoyment. As you can imagine, many people dream about playing in Carnegie Hall and my dream had come true."

He shared other details of this memorable experience with me. Then he turned to me and asked: "What has been your greatest experience?"

I told him that I had had some very memorable experiences in my life. One of them was when I graduated from college. After four years of hard work and many struggles, Mom and Dad were there when I got my diploma along with several awards including National Honor Society and Who's Who in American Colleges and Universities. I told him that it was a great moment when Mom and

Dad told me that they were very proud of me.

I then told him that what made this moment so special was that ten years before I had had an experience that helped me find meaning and purpose in life. Prior to this experience I was aware of a void and a yearning for significance as well as uncertainty about my future. For some reason I felt a sense of guilt and a fear of death.

I told him that it was at this time that I started reading the Bible and I found that Jesus said: *"I have come that you might have life and that you might have it more abundantly."* I then shared with him that following what the Bible said, I decided to invite Jesus into my life. "It was absolutely amazing," I said, "as I prayed I felt a sense of peace that I had never felt before."

I shared with him the story of Jesus and how a person can have this kind of relationship with Him. Throughout the conversation he listened very attentively and thanked me for sharing this experience with him.

While I cannot say that he made a decision to receive Christ during our conversation, I definitely had the opportunity to sow the seed of the Gospel with a person who otherwise might not have been willing to listen. Christian witnesses should be ever alert to the opportunities to share the Good News with those who inquire and provide opportunities for such sharing. Our own LifeStory can be a part of opening the door to such sharing. Witnesses can also use Bible stories to bridge or move to the story of Jesus.

Bridging Bible Stories

There are instances in which it is helpful to utilize a Bible story as a bridge before getting to the story of Jesus. The question, therefore, would be what Bible story connects best with the felt need of this person at this time? For the theme of joys and achievements some of the following stories may be appropriate:

- David and Goliath (1 Sa. 17)

- Esther (Es. 2-7)
- Shepherds and the Angels (Lu. 2)
- Jesus at the Wedding (Jn. 2)
- Jesus at the Home of Mary and Martha (Lu. 10)

You can undoubtedly find other Bible stories that will connect with this theme. Continue to think creatively and add them to this list.

Life-Shaping Influences

The second theme, life-shaping influences, is a most special one for many people. This theme provides them an opportunity to share some thoughts and honor those persons who have made a difference in their lives. Often people enjoy talking about people who have influenced their lives in a significant way. They will mention their mother, their father, a school teacher, a coach, a minister, a friend, or someone else who has made a major contribution to their lives through their influence.

Positive Influences

In most instances when people talk about life-shaping influences they speak about people who have had a positive influence on their lives. It is important as we listen to them to ask questions about the ways in which they were influenced by this person. This sharing then provides a very natural bridge for us to share how Jesus has had the greatest influence on our lives after we turned our lives over to him.

Example: A Canal Zone Pilot

When we were serving as missionaries in the Republic of Panama, my wife and I went frequently to see that Panama Canal and observe ships as they passed through a series of locks from one ocean to the other. Almost every time friends and relatives came to visit us, they wanted us to take them to see the canal. I listened to so many presentations on the operation of the canal locks that I could have made them myself.

One day, however, I had a very different experience. A Canal Zone Pilot took me on his small boat to the canal and explained to me how the pilot guides the ship through the locks from one ocean to the other. He told me that when a Ship Captain approaches the bay he reaches a certain point where he has to stop and wait for an official Canal Zone Pilot to come on board, take control of the ship, and guide it safely through the canal. He explained to me that often the center of the canal is not the deepest part, that there are landslides, and that the canal zone locks are so narrow for modern ships that only a highly trained Canal Zone Pilot can guide the ship safely through.

As the Canal Zone Pilot explained the procedures to me and visibly pointed out how he guided the ship, the thought came to my mind that that is exactly what Jesus has done in my life. He came into my life at a time when there was a lot of confusion, a lack of sense of direction, a number of key decisions which would determine the direction of my life, and a time in which there were clear dangers and difficult experiences ahead.

Jesus, who knew exactly where all the dangers and snares were, has had the greatest influence on my life by giving me a clear example to follow and a clear sense of direction. As I think of all of the bad decisions I could have made, all of the destructive actions I could have engaged in (drugs, gangs, etc.), I am grateful to the Lord that he has not only guided me in the past, but continues to guide me in every aspect of my life.

As I have reflected on these experiences of God's protection, the thought has come to mind of the story of Jesus being in the boat with his disciples and calming the storm. I thought that this story would be helpful in conveying the concept that we can trust Jesus with our lives and can count on him when we are assailed by the storms of life. The message of Jesus and his care for us and protection over us is a message greatly needed in our day.

Negative Influences

There are times when people in the course of telling their story bring up the subject of those who have hurt or humiliated them. This is an opportunity to minister to them by hearing their story sympathetically, sharing a slice of your LifeStory, and sharing with them the story of Jesus, who loves them dearly, can help them make peace with their past and can help them to rebuild their story.

Example: A Young Lady Contemplating Suicide

After I preached a sermon on the love of God, a young lady came and said she would like to talk with me. As we sat in my office she opened her purse and pulled out a bottle of pills. She explained: "I came to church this morning with the idea that if somehow I could not find a solution to my problem I would swallow the pills in this bottle and take my own life."

I enquired what problem was overwhelming her life.

She replied:

> Throughout my life I have felt a deep sense of rejection and anger on the part of my father. I was just a little girl when my brother was born with a congenital heart defect. I could sense that my parents were very worried about him. They told me not to do anything to upset him. He was about two years old when we started fighting over a toy that we both wanted. All of a sudden my little brother fell to the floor, started gasping for air, and before the ambulance could arrive he died. From that day on, every time my father got angry at me he would tell me: "You killed your brother, you killed your brother, and I will never forgive you." I have grown up with a deep sense of guilt and rejection. If I cannot find a way to deal with this I am going to kill myself.

I listened attentively and sympathetically and then offered to pray for her.

She agreed to let me pray for her but made one request: "When you pray for me don't use the word 'father,' because when I think of my father I think of a tyrant who hates me and rejects me."

I explained to her that our Heavenly Father is the exact opposite of that. I then shared with her the story of the prodigal son (which should actually be called the story of the loving father) and pointed out to her that God loved her, accepted her, and wanted to have a genuine fellowship with her.

She listened very attentively as I spoke and said she desperately needed the kind of love and acceptance that the father showed when he forgave his son. After further conversation, I prayed for her. She left my office with a smile on her face saying that she felt very happy knowing that God loved her.

These kinds of experiences await those who adopt the Bible Storying methods of proclaiming the Message of Jesus.

Bridging Stories

A good number of Bible stories connect with the theme of life-shaping influences. The following are just a few examples:

- Naomi and Ruth (Ruth)
- David and Jonathan (1 Samuel.)
- Jesus and Zaccheus (Luke 19)
- Jesus and Mary Magdalene (Matt 27, 28;
- John 20)
- Barnabas and John Mark (Acts, Epistles)
- Paul and Timothy (Acts, Epistles)

You will undoubtedly want to share the story of how Jesus has had the greatest influence on your life and the lives of others you know.

Sorrows and Difficulties

A third of the themes related to the LifeStories of people involve sorrows and difficulties they have encountered. Trouble touches every life eventually. These experiences may eventuate in vague unrest and sometimes in anguish so intense as to be almost unbearable. To some, trouble comes as an episode, while for others it seems to be permanent and pervasive in their lives. Sorrow and/or difficulty consist of physical pain, psychological confusion, or spiritual emptiness.

Often, if people are going through intense suffering, you do not have to ask them any questions to get them to talk about it; they will share their experiences spontaneously. If this is the case, you need to listen very carefully and sympathetically.

Example: A Worried Lady

I boarded a plane at Love Field in Dallas en route to Houston to train some young people how to share their faith. I was looking forward to reviewing my notes, but just to be courteous I turned to the woman sitting next to me and said: "Good afternoon, how are you?"

She looked at me and had some tears in her eyes when she said: "I'm not doing well. A car hit my Mom and I am not sure if she is going to be alive when I get there."

When I heard this I prayed silently that the Lord would help me to minister to her. I replied: "It is evident that your Mom means a lot to you."

She shared with me how her mother had loved her so much and how she had sacrificed so much in providing for her.

After listening to her for a while, I said: "Lady, I can empathize with you. I still remember when the doctor told my wife and me that our six-month old baby daughter had been diagnosed with leukemia." I added: "This was the saddest news I had ever heard in my life and caused the deepest pain I had ever experienced. My world came to a screeching halt and my only concern was my daughter's wellbeing."

Then I said: "I would have lost my mind if it hadn't been for the fact that the peace and the presence of Jesus were in my heart. He gave us the strength we needed from one checkup to another. We tried to make every day count and we have many wonderful memories. One night the angels came and took our daughter to heaven. I still remember walking into the hospital room and seeing my daughter's lifeless body on the bed. But I also remember that the presence of Jesus was so real in my heart that I felt strength and a comfort that I had never felt in that measure before. My wife and I ended up comforting our loved ones during the funeral, not because we were trying to be heroic, but because Jesus was with us in a special way."

The lady answered, "I wish I had the peace that you are talking about." I replied: "You can have it by receiving Jesus, the Prince of Peace in your heart." I then told her the story of Jesus and how he died on the cross to save us of our sins and to guide us during the most difficult moments of our lives. The flight from Dallas Love Field to Houston Hobby Airport took only 45 minutes, but when the plane was landing, she was praying to receive Christ. As we made our way off the plane, she took me by the arm and said: "God put you in my path. I had missed my first flight and was beside myself. Now I know why. Thank you for talking to me about Jesus. I know that he is going to be with me."

During the course of the conversation I was able to get her address so I wrote a pastor in her city to continue to minister to her. This lady's need was so poignant that it didn't take long for us to start communicating at the heart-to-heart level. Even though it is always difficult for me to share my thoughts and emotions regarding my daughter's death, doing so in this case provided a bridge through which we could communicate. We should become willing to share our experiences even when the sharing is difficult as God can use these accounts to reach others.

Bridging Bible Stories

Many stories in the Bible connect with the theme of sorrows and difficulties. The following provide a brief listing of some of these stories:

- The Story of Joseph (Genesis)
- The Escape of Mary, Joseph and Jesus to Egypt (Matt 2)
- Jesus Calms the Storm (Matt 8)
- Jesus Walks on Water (Matt 14)
- Jesus Heals the Man Born Blind (John 9)
- Jesus Heals the Demon Possessed Boy (Matt 17)
- Jesus Raises Lazarus (John 11)

The Bible contain a large number of stories dealing with sorrows and difficulties. This body of stories makes it possible for you to select the ones that relate to the specific sorrow or difficulty that the person with whom you are conversing is experiencing. You can select a story that meets the person's needs. Experiences with persons who are experiencing sorrows and difficulties provide unique ministry opportunities.

Changes and Challenges

A fourth theme often seen in the lives of persons who are telling their stories relates to the matter of changes and challenges. Every life has peaks and valleys. No life is a progressive climb upward without dips, gullies, and plateaus. When people are on the crest of the wave they feel full of life, excitement, and anticipation. When they are in the valley they experience boredom, restlessness, confusion, depression, and anger.

Transition is brought about by the experience of loss of physical vitality through illness or accident, the loss of a spouse or a friend, the loss of a job or an opportunity, or the sense of loss when their children leave home. People get the feeling that their world will never be the same again. Transition at times results in an increase in status or power or new relationships.

Whether positive or negative, transition can bring anxiety and confusion. Studies indicate that transition is also a time when people can become more receptive to the gospel because they are looking for new ways to cope with the change that has occurred in their lives. Witnesses can be aware of these transitions and make use of them in sharing the Message of Jesus.

Example: A Young Lady Starting A New Career

I had been in Singapore for a week conducting a church growth seminar. Due to my heavy schedule and jet lag, I was not in the mood to witness to anyone as I boarded the plane to return to the United States. My attitude was: "Lord, I don't want to talk to anyone. I just want to be left alone and catch up on my sleep. If I have to witness, let it be somebody easy."

I felt safe as I sat next to a Chinese young lady assuming that she was going to be typically reserved. To my surprise, she stuck out her hand and said: "Hello, my name is Vivian, what is your name?"

After we introduced ourselves she told me that she was on her way to New York City to work with an advertising agency. I told her that I used to live in New York and I gave her some tips on how to survive in the Big Apple.

After additional conversation I said: "I have a daughter named Vivian and you know what my greatest wish is when she gets to be your age and takes on a challenge such as the one you are taking?" She answered: "I am very interested in knowing what you wish for her is." I said: "My wish is that she is going to have such a strong faith in Jesus that she is going to be full of confidence knowing that no matter what she faces she can count on him for strength and guidance."

"Oh", she said, "you must be a Christian." She added: "My parents are Buddhist, but I have some Christian friends and I try to pray to God. Do you think I am doing the right thing?"

This opened the door wide open for me to tell her the story of Jesus. She listened very attentively, asked questions, and told me she was going to think very seriously about what I had told her. I gave her my Bible and mailed her some recorded songs because she said she enjoyed listening to them.

While she did not make a decision for Christ during our conversation, this may have been one of a series of conversations that hopefully contributed toward her coming to a personal faith in Him. In this case it was her conversation about her transition that opened the way for me to share with her in a very natural and cordial way about the Lord. In a sense we went from her story, to my daughter's story and then to His story.

Example: A Man Adjusting To Life In A New City

On Good Friday we did not have classes at the seminary so I decided to spend the day reflecting on the death of our Savior Jesus Christ and preparing some church starting training sessions that I was scheduled to conduct in a conference. Remembering that this was also a time that I needed to get the brakes on my car repaired, I took some books with me to read while the brakes were under repair. When I talked to the manager I found out that I was going to need to leave my car there but that one of the workers could take me home and later pick me up.

When I got in the pickup truck, the driver greeted me and told me his name was Andrés. As we began our trip he asked me if I had gotten a day off. "Yes," I replied, "I am very happy that I was able to take the day off and to meditate about the very important event that took place on Holy Friday when Jesus died for us on the cross."

He answered: "I did not get the day off and I am having to work very hard these days." He then told me that he had recently arrived in Fort Worth and that he was fortunate to find a job at this repair shop.

I asked him how he liked living in Fort Worth and he said he was beginning to get used to it but was having to work long hours just to make a living.

I then replied, "I'm sure that there are times when you wonder if there is more to life than just working to earn a living."

"Yes," he said, "I wonder sometimes."

I then told him: "You know, there was a time when as a young man I really wondered about the meaning of life." "Like the Spanish Poet, Unamuno, I asked myself, 'what was I born for.' Around that time someone gave me a Bible, God's Word, and one of the things that got my attention was when Jesus said: 'I have come so that you can have a full and meaningful life.' The more I read the Gospel of John, the more I found out that I needed to repent of my sins and invite Jesus (in a spiritual way) into my life.

One night I knelt and asked Jesus to come into my heart and immediately I felt a peace that I had never felt before and a certainty that I was going to be with Jesus when I died." Just about this time we arrived at my home and he said he would come back for me when the car was ready.

When he came back, I got in the car and, before we started the trip back, I gave him a copy of the New Testament. I said: "I have a gift for you. This is a portion of the Word of God and I would like to recommend to you that you start with the Gospel of John and, as a matter of fact, I have put a tab on the portion that tells us how Jesus died for us on the cross."

He said: "I know that all religions are good. I lean toward the Catholic Church but I respect other religions."

I replied: "The Catholic Church has wonderful teachings that come straight out of the Bible. As you know it teaches that God is our Creator, that Jesus, His Son, was born of the Virgin Mary, that he taught us through his example and his teachings, and that he died on the cross for our sins. If we repent of our sins and invite him into our lives, he will forgive us and give us a life full of purpose and meaning. The Bible says that God loves us so much that he sent his Son to die for us."

Then he said, "You are not going to believe this, but one day I cried out to God. I was riding a tractor and all of a sudden it hit a stump, threw me over, and pinned me against a brick wall. As one of the wheels of the tractor was turning and pushing me against the wall it tore my clothes off and I was about to pass out because I could not breathe. At that moment I asked God to help me. And, you're not going to believe this, but the motor of the tractor stopped and the wheel stopped turning. Some people finally saw me and were able to free me up. The space between the wheel and the wall was so small that I don't know how I was able to survive and even walk away without any broken bones."

I then asked: "Do you think that was a miracle?"

"Yes," he said, "it had to be a miracle."

Then I asked: "Do you think that God loves you and has a purpose for your life?"

"Yes, I think he does," he answered, "and I am going to read this book that you have given me."

By this time we were back at the repair shop and as he got out of the car he again thanked me for talking with him and for giving him the New Testament. Since I will be going back to get the brakes adjusted I will again seek opportunities to continue my conversation with him.

It was rather interesting that while at first he seemed very friendly he appeared to be a bit hesitant to talk about spiritual matters. As time went on, however, he felt comfortable sharing his story which gave me the opportunity to talk more about The Story. In this case, being that it was Good Friday, it was very natural to start with the story of the crucifixion. That, along with the conversation, paved the way for him to share his story which in turn gave me an idea of where he was spiritually.

Bridging Bible Stories

The following Bible stories can connect with the theme of changes and challenges:

- Joseph (Book of Genesis)
- David and Goliath (1 Sam 17)
- Esther (Book of Esther)
- Daniel (Book of Daniel)
- Jesus Overcomes Temptations (Matt 4)
- The Prodigal Son (Luke 15)

As you have noticed, some Bible stories can be used to connect with several themes. For example, the story of Joseph can be used to connect with the themes of joys and victories, changes and challenges, as well as sorrows and difficulties. The story of the Prodigal Son also connects with several themes, even some that relate to felt needs and values as we will explain later in this chapter. Again, pray for the Lord's wisdom and guidance as you select these stories.

I will never forget the military officer in Guatemala who said after I had told the story of the Prodigal Son, "Today you told my story and I want to come back to the Father." That is what we pray for. Therefore, continue to seek the Lord's guidance and to think creatively as you review Bible stories and keep them fresh in your mind for the moment when they will be exactly what a person needs to hear in order to draw near to the Lord.

Observations

What is the best way to prepare for these types of LifeStory Encounters?

1. Pray that the Lord will prepare you spiritually so that you will be in the best position possible to share the good news of salvation. Ask the Lord to empower you ahead of time for every opportunity.

2. Be sensitive to the people around you and those you meet even unexpectedly. Some may be sending a distress signal and you may not be picking up on it.

3. Don't worry if you have not had an experience similar to the one the person shares with you. Simply listen sympathetically and state that you cannot imagine what it is like to go through that type of experience. You can then assure the person that your experience with Christ gives you the confidence that He can be with that person in the experience through which he or she is going.

4. Place that person in the hands of the Lord and continue to pray for him or her that the Word of God will not return void. The sharing opportunity does not end with the final words of your conversation.

5. Prepare in advance. Time spent reviewing your own LifeStory, reading anew the Bible stories, and reflecting on which ones you would use in each situation will be very valuable in preparing you for the moment when you are face to face with the person that God has arranged for you to witness to. With that in mind, focus on the following suggestions.

Suggestions on Methods

Write Your LifeStory

Write brief "slice of life testimonies." Often in sharing our Life Story it is neither necessary nor desirable for us to tell our entire story. We can decide to focus on the slice of our Life Story that connects more closely with the Life Story that the person has shared with us. For example, if the person shares a story which focuses on grief, we can select of slice of our life in which we have experienced grief.

We can use the same procedure in relation to some of the themes that we have already mentioned (e.g., change, joy, life-shaping influence, sorrow). We can, therefore, share what we have gone through and focus on the difference Christ made in our lives as we faced these experiences. This sharing will communicate to the person that Christ can make a difference in his or her life and can then open the door to share the story of Jesus in a way that connects with the story of the person with whom we are conversing.

Focus on One of the Themes Listed Below or Others that Come to Mind.

Joys and Achievements

1. Describe my experience.
2. Describe the difference having a personal relationship with Christ made.
3. Show how Christ can make a difference in the life of someone else.

Life-Shaping Influences

1. Describe my experience

2. Describe the difference having a personal relationship with Christ made.
3. Show how Christ can make a difference in the life of someone else.

Sorrows and Difficulties

1. Describe my experience.
2. Describe the difference having a personal relationship with Christ made.
3. Show how Christ can make a difference in the life of someone else.

Changes and Challenges

1. Describe my experience.
2. Describe the difference having a personal relationship with Christ made.
3. Show how Christ can make a difference in the life of someone else.

Other Themes?

1. Describe my experience.
2. Describe the difference having a personal relationship with Christ made.
3. Show how Christ can make a difference in the life of someone else.

Practice Your LifeStory Testimony with Some of Your Close Christian Friends

1. Make sure you don't use a lot of "theological" or in-church expressions.
2. Make it brief

3. Describe your experience enough to establish rapport with the person you want to witness to but be sure to focus on Christ.

Engage in LifeStory Encounters

There are two principal ways in which we can pave the way to share our LifeStory and then The Story:

Simply listening to people

Many times as we engage people in conversation, they will mention an experience that they have had or are having that falls under the broad categories of the four themes discussed below. This will often open the door for us to share with them an experience related to a similar theme and explain how our personal faith in Christ made the greatest difference in the world.

Asking Questions that Show Personal Concern

If people do not take the initiative to talk about one of these themes, we can ask them questions in a very friendly and natural way, that give people an opportunity to share some of their experiences. A list of suggested questions will be given under each of the themes.

Joys and Achievements

1. What is the best thing that happened to you in the last year? Why was it good?
2. What are the most meaningful achievements in your life?
3. What do you do for fun?
4. What things do you do well?
5. What are the three high points in your marriage? (Family?)
6. How would you complete this sentence: "It would give me real happiness to...."

Life-Shaping Influences

1. Look back through your life at the people who have influenced you most. Name two or three of them.
2. What were they like?
3. What values did they seem to live by?
4. What did you learn from them?
5. How are you alike or different from them?

Often people will bring up the subject of those who have hurt or humiliated them. This revelation often provides an opportunity to minister to them by introducing them to Jesus, the friend who always loves them. Perhaps some of the following questions can contribute to a healing conversation.

1. Have you found a way to forgive them?
2. How strong an influence do they still have on you?
3. How much of your energy is still being spent on nursing the hurt that you experienced through them?

Sorrows and Difficulties

Often if people are going through intense suffering you do not have to ask them any questions to get them to talk about it, they will do it spontaneously. If this is the case, you need to listen very carefully and sympathetically. Asking some of the following questions may be helpful.

1. How is this affecting you and your family?
2. How are coping?
3. On whom are you depending as a source of strength and comfort?
4. How can we help you at this time?

Changes and Challenges

When people are going through transition, they may be excited or scared or both. What may appear to be a wonderful opportunity for advancement may also carry with it changes (residence, friendships, associates, etc.) that are worrisome to the person. Having someone to talk to about these changes can be very helpful and reassuring for the person experiencing these.

Some of the following questions can be useful:

1. How do you feel about this change?
2. What excites you about it?
3. Is there anything that worries you about it?
4. What are you depending on to help you make this transition successfully?

CHAPTER 2

INSPIRING LIFESTORY ENCOUNTERS

Daniel R. Sánchez

The Bible records a number of significant divine appointments in which the good news of salvation was communicated and people responded by placing their faith in Christ. Several of these divine appointments show the use of stories in the communication process. Christians today can draw inspiration and guidance from the ways biblical witnesses used stories to proclaim the gospel of Christ.

Biblical Examples of Encounters

Philip was in Samaria leading what we might call a "city-wide revival." Large numbers of Samaritans were receiving Christ as their personal savior, turning from a life of sin and witchcraft, and being baptized into the fellowship of the Church (Acts 8:11, 12). The Apostles Peter and John had been sent by the Jerusalem Church to check out this gospel-proclaiming meeting. Right in the middle of that marvelous revival meeting, the Holy Spirit sent Philip to the desert (v. 27).

In spite of the fact that from a human perspective it made absolutely no sense to leave Samaria at that time, Philip obeyed and made his way to the desert. Lo and behold, the Holy Spirit instructed him to draw near to a chariot in which a man was reading from a scroll. What were the chances that someone from another country just happened to be reading from Isaiah 53?

Philip started with a very pertinent question: "Do you understand what you are reading?" The Ethiopian man invited Philip on board and enquired of whom the prophet was speaking. In response to that question, Philip did some "fast-track storying" starting from that portion of Isaiah and sharing with the Ethiopian man the story of Jesus.

We know that rest of the story that the man who was an official in the Queen's court in Ethiopia received Christ, was baptized, and returned to his homeland. Some historians believe that the Ethiopian man may have been the first to introduce the gospel to the continent of Africa. How important was that?

Paul, in his eagerness to spread the gospel to fulfill the Great Commission, made careful plans to go to Bithynia but the Holy Spirit had other plans (Acts 16: 7-10). Through a vision the Holy Spirit instructed him to go instead to Macedonia. When Paul and his companion arrived in the Macedonian city, Philippi, they encountered a business woman named Lydia who was meeting with other women for prayer along the riverside (v.14). When Lydia heard the message, she received Christ in her heart and invited Paul and Silas to her home where they shared the good news with her family. Lydia and her household were baptized (v. 15).

The spiritual victory was not, however, the end of the story. When Paul and Silas were released from jail, they went to Lydia's home where she and the believers were gathered (v. 38). This was not only the beginning of the church at Philippi but also marked the introduction of the gospel to that part of the continent of Europe. How important was that?

These encounters initially might appear to be chance meetings. Actually these meetings were divine appointments guided by the Holy Spirit for the furtherance of the Gospel to very strategic people and places. Is the Holy Spirit not still in the business of setting up divine appointments? Many of us can point to instances that might seem chance encounters but which, seen in retrospective, have convinced us that they had to be the work of God.

Present-Day Examples of Encounters

By sharing the following experiences, we want to encourage you to be sensitive to the working of the Holy Spirit in setting up these appointments. We also hope to help you be prepared in order that, like Philip and Paul, you can be an instrument in the hands of God to share the message of salvation to people with whom he is already working. We want to remind you that only eternity will be able to measure the total impact of your witness if you are willing to share it when the Lord leads you.

The following are additional examples of experiences I have had in listening to someone's story, sharing my story, and telling The Story (of Jesus). You will notice that even though many of the elements of these encounters may be similar, there is not a "perfect pattern." People are different one from another. They have a wide variety of experiences some of which are quite unique to them. The important thing is not to try to follow a strict pattern but to be flexible in the way you engage in the LifeStory Encounter and be sensitive to the guidance of the Holy Spirit.

A Young Man Searching for Purpose in Life

I had just concluded two days of teaching a concentrated course in Nuevo Laredo, Mexico, when I boarded the airplane to return to Fort Worth. I was delighted that the students had been so receptive yet my thoughts turned quickly to a conference I was going to lead in California. As I sat next to a young man I prayed silently, "Lord, if you want me to witness to this young man, please open a way for me to do it." Even though I prayed this prayer my preference would have been to work on my pending conference.

When I greeted the young man (Isaac) he was very friendly. As the plane took off, Isaac began to take a nap. As soon as we were given the okay sign, I took out my computer and started to work on my conference presentation. I hadn't worked more than 10 minutes when Isaac said: "Please pardon my intrusion, but what is the Hellenistic Analogy that you have on your computer screen?" I replied: "Well, Hellenistic is actually a term applied to Hebrew people in the Bible who had assimilated to a certain degree into the Greek culture."

Isaac paused for a moment and said: "You know, this causes me to wonder about something. I grew up in a very conservative Roman Catholic home in Mexico. Recently, I moved to El Paso, Texas. How do you think my children are going to adjust being Catholic but living in this country?"

I replied: "Because your children are learning English in school, very likely they may want to go to an English-speaking mass in the future. Also, it is quite possible that they will have friends who are not Catholic."

"I can certainly understand that," he answered, "because most or my friends are 'Christians.'"

"That's very interesting," I replied.

"Yes," he said, "and they are actually very good people."

I then got back to the original question and said: "So basically what you are concerned about is your children retaining their religious and cultural values as they adjust to life in this country."

"Yes," he said, "that's exactly right. My parents would be very disappointed if they lost these values and I would too."

I then said, "You know, Isaac, these values must be ingrained in us if we are going to transmit them to our children. As a very young man I had a very strong yearning to find purpose and meaning in life. It was then that I started reading the Bible, especially the Gospel of St. John. There I found a statement by Jesus that said 'I have come that you might have life and have it abundantly.' As I continued to read, I found out that in order to have this life full of meaning and purpose I needed to invite Jesus into my life in a spiritual way. When I prayed a prayer inviting Jesus to come into my heart, forgive me of my sins, and guide my life, I immediately felt a peace that I had never felt before."

"That is very interesting," he said, "because I know that all of us have a desire to find real purpose in life."

Then I continued telling him that what had helped my wife and me to communicate these values to our children was to tell them stories from the Bible from the time that they were very young. I then said: "You know, something that is very interesting is that our oldest son, who is a commercial designer, has recently played the part of a modern Prodigal Son in a film produced by the Salvation Army. As a matter of fact, I have some pictures of him here on my computer."

As I showed him the pictures I told him the parable of the Prodigal Son. I then said, "You know, I have my Bible with me, do you mind if we read this story from God's Word?" He enthusiastically agreed. He listened very attentively and then said: "The teaching appears to be that even if we mess up, if we repent, God will forgive us and receive us back as his children."

I said: "that's exactly right."

He then said, "This is a great story because it lets us know that we can start over if we make mistakes."

Just about this time we were landing and he asked for my e-mail address so that he could stay in touch with me. As he left the airplane he said: "God must have made our meeting possible because I learned so much from you today." As I reflected on this I fully agreed with him that this had been a divine appointment.

A Grieving Mother

I had just finished my last summer school exam at the seminary and I decided to do something different. For some time I had been curious about Lee Harvey Oswald's grave at a cemetery in Fort Worth so I decided to see if I could find it. When I got to the cemetery one of the caretakers was kind enough to point me in the right direction.

When I arrived at the graveside, I noticed that an elderly lady was watering the grass over the grave. Having seen her picture on television, I immediately recognized her as Margaret Oswald, Lee Harvey's mother. I walked up and introduced myself telling her that I was as student at Southwestern Seminary. She replied: "Well, this is very interesting. When my son was killed the only minister who came to visit me was from your seminary. This seemed to open the door for she immediately became very talkative.

For about thirty minutes she talked to me about her son's innocence. She shared with me several theories about others who had plotted to assassinate President Kennedy. She told me about her testimony to the Warren Commission and how she had pointed out to them that the President had been killed as a result of a conspiracy and that her son was made the scapegoat. Every once in a while she would say: "My son was a good boy; he could not have killed the president."

Then she said: "Because you are from the seminary, I think that you will understand what I am going to tell you." She continued: "On the Sunday that Lee Harvey was shot and killed by Jack Ruby there was a service at the National Cathedral in Washington, DC." "Young man," she continued, "at that service they prayed for Mrs. Rose Kennedy, for Jackie and the children, and they even prayed for the widow of officer Tippet who was killed in Dallas." Then tears welled up in her eyes when she said: "But they did not pray for me and at that hour, I needed God too."

I must confess that my initial emotional reaction to Mrs. Oswald had been one of anger because she was the mother of the man who shot the President that I admired so much. Listening to her say that she "needed God" brought a feeling of compassion. Here was a grieving mother watering the grass over her son's grave and sharing the deep sorrow and loneliness that she had experienced in connection with her son's death. At that moment she was very open to hearing that God is willing to draw near to us if we open our hearts to him and that Jesus made it a point to comfort people who had lost loved ones like the widow who had lost her son.

After we had conversed for about an hour, she decided to roll up the water hose and leave for home. Before she did, she thanked me for being willing to listen to her and for sharing with her words of comfort.

She then said, "See that car that's parked over there? They are law officers and they follow me everywhere I go." When she drove off in her car, sure enough they followed her.

Some of the theories she shared with me about the President's assassination were later verbalized in a movie and in a Senate Committee that conducted an extensive investigation. I cannot say that I agreed with her on any of these theories. What I can say is that by listening to her story and hearing her story opened up the way for us to converse at a heart to heart level. Such heart-to-heart conversation often opens the way to share relevant biblical stories that provide bridges for the communication of the Gospel story. We should remain open to the opportunities that such encounters give us to share the Good News of Jesus with lost people.

A Guilt-laden Young Man

When I was a missionary in the Republic of Panama, a young man came to my office and asked if he could speak with me. My first impression was that he was a homeless person. His hair was uncombed, his clothing was not clean, and he had a bewildered look on his face.

He started out by saying: "My friend told me that you could help me and I hope you can because my life is a nightmare."

I replied: "Well, tell me about your life."

He then told me one of the saddest stories I have ever heard.

He said, "My mother died when she was giving birth to me. As a little boy one of the first things I remember hearing my father say to me was, 'you killed your mother, I hate you.' I grew up feeling very guilty and very sorry about killing my mother whom I had never seen. To get rid of me my father sent me to an orphanage. I stayed there for a few years but I felt very guilty and very lonely. One day I left the orphanage and started living in the streets because none of my relatives wanted me to live with them."

Then he looked at me with a very piercing look and said: "Sir, I have committed every sin you can imagine, do you think God can forgive me?"

I responded by telling him that God loved him so much that he sent his Son Jesus to die on the cross to pay for his sin. I then told him that the Bible says that the blood of Jesus Christ cleanses us from all of our sins.

He replied: "But you have no idea of all the sins I have committed. Can God really forgive me?"

I said: "The Bible says that because of the sacrifice of Jesus on the cross, if we truly repent of our sins, God will forgive us."

He then asked: "What do I need to do?"

I replied: "Let us both kneel down on the floor here and you start the prayer by asking God to forgive you of your sins. When you are through, I will pray and thank God that he has forgiven you."

When we knelt, this young man started to cry out, "Oh God, Oh God, I have committed many sins, please forgive me. I want to invite Jesus into my life." As he was sobbing his body was shaking and the tears were flowing. When he ended his prayer, I prayed thanking God for forgiving this young man.

When we stood up, his face was bathed with tears, yet there was a smile on his face. He said: "I don't know what has happened but I have a peace in my heart that I have never felt before." This man went on to be one of the evangelical youth leaders in the Republic of Panama and was instrumental in starting several churches. His testimony became a powerful tool for proclamation of the Gospel. Every time I saw him I was reminded of the transforming power of the Gospel Story.

A Deeply-Troubled Young Lady

When I boarded the plane in Corpus Christi, Texas, I had already had a very long day. Early that morning I had left from Love Field in Dallas en route to Houston and then to Corpus Christi. From there I had rented a car to drive to Kingsville to attend the inauguration for the President of Texas A & I University. As I sat on board the airplane for my return flight, I was so tired that I was glad that the only empty seat in the whole airplane with next to me.

Just before the door of the airplane closed low and behold there was a young lady walking in the direction of the empty seat. When I looked at her I thought that she had fallen face first into a tackle box. She had multiple hooks (or earrings) on her eyebrows, on her ears, on her nose, and even one through her tongue. My first thought was, "Lord, what have I done to deserve this. I am going to have to sit next to this creature during this entire flight."

When she sat down, just to be courteous I said: "Good afternoon, how are you doing?"

She took a deep breath and said: "I'm not doing well at all. Last week my boyfriend committed suicide. This week I found out that I am pregnant. Yesterday I fell down and broke my arm. Today I called my parents and they said they don't want to see me."

Then I took a deep breath and prayed silently: "Lord, help me to minister to this young lady. I don't know where or how to start."

I then looked at her and said: "I don't know that I can even begin to imagine how badly you must be feeling. I have never met anyone who was hit by so many problems all at once." I then continued: "All I can tell you is that when I have had to face problems and disappointments it has been very helpful for me to read God's Word and to pray and to cry out to Him for help."

Picking up on the theme of her feeling rejected by her parents I said: "You know, many times we as human parents are so overwhelmed by the problems of our children that we respond in very negative ways. There is one father who loves us so much that he is willing to forgive us if we repent and to receive us back as if we had not offended him."

She looked at me with a puzzled expression on her face as if she were asking, "who is this father?"

I said: "I am talking about God, our heavenly Father. The Bible says that God loved us so much that he sent his Son, Jesus, to come to earth and die on the cross so that we could be forgiven of our sins. There came a time in my life when I realized that many things I had done had offended God. I then told God that I was sorry for my sins and that I wanted to invite Jesus to come into my life to guide me and to give me strength to live for him."

She said: "I've gone to church a few times but I have never read the Bible."

I replied: "Let me encourage you to start reading the Bible. In it you are going to find the stories of many people who had many problems but when they put their faith in Jesus, he changed their lives."

The trip from Corpus Christi to Houston is a short one. As we were landing I asked her if I could pray for her. She said: "Yes, please pray for me." I then put my hand on her hand and prayed that God would help and that he would enable her to feel his love and presence as she faced those overwhelming problems in her life. I also prayed that she would start reading the Bible and find people who could help her to get close to God.

As she was getting into the isle she turned around and said: "Thank you for talking to me." The way she said it she sounded as if I had done her a big favor by just listening to her and conversing with her.

I regret that I did not have a Bible or even a tract to give her so I did the best I could under the circumstances. My greatest concern, however, as I reflected on this experience was that initially I had been judgmental and unconcerned.

My prayer is that this LifeStory encounter somehow planted the seed of the gospel and that someone else was able to water and cultivate the seed in the life of this young lady with such desperate needs. I also pray that even when I am weary and want to be left alone, I will be open enough to the work of the Holy Spirit to recognize the divine appointments that he has made for me.

A Surprised Translator

Not long after the breakup of the Soviet Union I was invited to go to the city of Khabarovsk in Eastern Russia. A good portion of the trip was for the purpose of surveying the fields and learning about opportunities for missionary work in that part of the world.

Due to the fact that neither I nor my two fellow missionaries knew how to speak Russian, we were assigned a translator by the name of Tatiana. Even though Tatiana was not a believer, she was very friendly and very helpful as a translator. The fact that she taught English at the Pedagogical School (Teachers College) in the city enabled her to translate accurately and fluently.

During our stay we interviewed a number of Russian Christians and visited some of the churches. On a very cold Saturday morning (zero degrees) we boarded a train to go to a small town. When we got there the taxi driver who picked us up was the pastor of a small, yet very old church. As we arrived at the church we noticed that it was packed full. When we got to the platform each one of us was asked to preach.

We were also asked to sing. Aware of the fact that Russian Christians have been acquainted with the song "How Great Thou Art," I suggested that we sing it. We, the visitors, then stood up and started to sing the first stanza in English. To our surprise when we got to the chorus, the entire congregation stood up and joined us as they sang in Russian. Thinking of all the persecutions and sufferings they had endured in the past made this moment very special for their song was a testimony of God's power and presence which they had experienced in their lives as Christians.

When the time came for me to preach, I decided to preach a narrative sermon on the Prodigal Son. Tatiana, my interpreter, was doing a marvelous job. Even though I did not understand the language I could sense that she was very fluent and that the congregation was listening very attentively. Everything was flowing very smoothly until I got to the point in the story when the prodigal son returns and the father received him. I said: "And the father ran and embraced his son."

Suddenly there was silence on the part of Tatiana. I thought to myself, perhaps I need to use another word so I said: "And the father ran and hugged his son." Still there was silence. I then said: "So the father ran out and put his arms around his son." And still there was silence on the part of my interpreter. Finally, after a very long pause, Tatiana said something. I then continued the story and Tatiana did a marvelous job translating fluently all the way through to the end.

On the way back on board the train Tatiana said to me: "I'm sure that you noticed my long pause after you said that the father embraced his son."

I replied: "Yes, I did and I apologize for using some words that perhaps you were not acquainted with."

She answered: "It was not the words at all." Then, after a long pause, she asked me: "Did the father really forgive his son?" She then explained: "When you said that the father embraced his son, it was not that I didn't know the word, I just couldn't speak, and I was all choked up. I was so overwhelmed by the fact that the father was able to forgive and receive his son after all those terrible things he had done that I couldn't get the words out of my mouth."

She then told me the story of the struggles that she and her husband had had with their son who had totally ignored all of their sacrifices on his behalf and was living a life of rebellion and isolation. She said: "I wish that he would repent." "If he did," however, "I don't know if we could forgive him and take him back into our family."

This gave me the opportunity to talk about the fact that God loves us so much that if we repent of our sins (as the prodigal son did), he will not only forgive us but will restore us as his children. Tatiana, having been raised in an atheistic society and not having heard the story of salvation, still had to think through the things she had heard that afternoon.

It was interesting to me to observe that perhaps what logical arguments and orderly discussions of issues might not have been able to accomplish, the story of the prodigal son did. It seemed to cut through all of her intellectual defenses and reached the very depth of her soul. Bible stories will do that.

Concerned Parents

In 1978 the Cold War was still on. Many Americans were still quite concerned about a nuclear strike by the Soviet Union. Nikita Khrushchev had come to the United Nations and in one of the sessions had taken off his shoe and pounded on the table proclaiming to America: "We will bury you."

The Russians had invaded Afghanistan and most of us here in America felt that we could not trust them.

At this juncture of history, the dictators in the Soviet Union were exercising strict control over their communication systems. It was at this time that Dr. Elias Golonka, minister of the Southern Baptist Convention to the United Nations, and I decided to invite four Russian reporters (from the Pravda and Tass News Agencies) to a meal just before Christmas.

We were greatly surprised when they accepted our invitation. They, however, insisted that we not eat at the United Nations cafeteria but in some restaurant away from the UN Building. We thought it likely that they were concerned about listening devices that would reveal the content of our conversation. We gladly agreed with their request and walked several blocks to a Chinese Restaurant.

As we sat there waiting for the waiter to come we began to get acquainted. We started with a safe subject by talking about our families. In the course of the conversation I asked them what their greatest concern was in living in America with their families. To my surprise they stated that they were greatly concerned about the social pressure and the threats against their children, especially since the Russian invasion of Afghanistan.

I must confess that I felt the same distrust and contempt most Americans felt toward Russians at that time. At the same time, I started to feel a sense of empathy with them related to their concern for their children. At that moment I decided to lay aside for a while all our ideological differences and to relate to these Russian reporters strictly on a human level asking myself: "How would I as a parent feel if my children were being threatened." Both Dr. Golonka and I expressed our regret that their children were being threatened.

The conversation reached a deeper level when Dr. Golonka asked them what it was that had attracted them to a Marxist ideology. Each one of them told a story of the training they had received in their schools in Russia and how they had developed a strong idealism that through socialism they could make our world a much better place for everyone. They spoke of the benefits of a classless society in which everyone enjoyed the same status and benefits. They also spoke about the fact that they had been taught that belief in God was a way to keep poor people from aspiring for a better life in this world. They said that that was one of the reasons why they were atheists.

Both Dr. Golonka and I listened very attentively and asked questions to come to a better understanding of their personal stories. Dr. Golonka then told his story.

He said, "I was born in Poland. While I was still a very young man, my parents were killed when the Nazi armies invaded our country. I was able to escape and find safety in a refugee camp. While there I came in contact with young people who were committed to a Marxist ideology and I embraced that ideology. Even though my parents had been devout members of the Eastern Orthodox Church, I had concluded that belief in God and religion were matters only for ignorant and weak people.

As time went on, however, I began to see that the ideal of Marxism was not being reached and Marxist governments had created a privileged class for the members of the Communist Party. Furthermore, there was a void in my life that nothing was able to fill. It was at that time that someone gave me a Bible.

As I started reading I began to see evidence of the fact that there is a Supreme Being who created the world and us as human beings. I also read that this Supreme Being, God, loved us so much that he sent his Son, Jesus to die on the cross for our sins. It was then that I decided to let the teachings of Jesus guide my life and the spirit of Jesus fill the longing of my heart. When I did this, I felt a peace and a sense of purpose that surpassed any idealism that I had in the past. That is why today I am a Christian.[15]

The Russian reporters listened very attentively as Dr. Golonka shared his story with them but did not give any outward sign of being interested in what he had said. The conversation then turned to other topics related to their families and their adjustment to life in this country. As we were walking back to the

U.N. building one of the reporters slowed down to get away from his colleagues. He then approached me and asked: "Would it be possible for you to get me a Russian Bible?" I told him that I would be happy to do so.

Later in the day when I shared this with Dr. Golonka privately he told me that another one of the reporters had spoken to him when they were by themselves and had asked: "Would you get me a recording of the Christmas Song 'The Drummer Boy,' I would like for my family to listen to it during this season." Dr. Golonka took a Russian Bible to the reporter who had asked for one. Somehow, the others found out about it because one by one, they all asked for Russian Bibles.

The lesson I learned from this experience was that differences in the cultural, religious, or ideological background of people do not prevent us from connecting with them. No matter what the differences, if we connect with them on a human level and listen to their stories the time will come when they will listen to our stories and then The Story.

An Angry Sibling

It was a long flight from Atlanta to San Francisco. From time to time I would get up and walk to the back of the airplane just to stretch my legs. On one of these walks I noticed that one of the flight attendants was writing a letter. Simply to strike up a conversation I asked her: "Are you catching up on your correspondence?"

She looked up at me and said: "This is the saddest letter I've ever written in my whole life."

Almost not knowing how to respond to this unexpected comment I replied: "Sounds like a very important letter."

"It is," she replied, "I'm writing my Dad and telling him that if he lets my spoiled sister come back to our home, I will no longer be his daughter." She continued: "My sister is a tramp. Every time she gets dumped by one of the boyfriends with whom she has been living, she calls my Dad asking him to bail her out financially and to let her move in with us again." She added: "My problem is that Dad always pays more attention to her than to any of us in the family and he is always willing to help her after she has wasted his money on drugs and partying." She continued: "That is why I have decided to let my Dad choose between us. If he chooses her, I will move out and forget that I have a father. He is just not fair to the rest of us in the family."

At that moment I prayed for wisdom to know how to respond to her. I told her: "You know, as human parents we are not perfect and make many mistakes. I have a young son and a baby daughter and I confess to you that at times I have to be very careful not to be totally partial to my daughter. But, you know, there is a father who is always fair and impartial."

She replied: "There is? I sure would like to meet him."

I replied: "Actually I am talking about our Father in heaven." This then opened up the opportunity for me to talk with her about God's love for her. At the end of the brief conversation she thanked me for taking the time to talk with her about someone who really loves her.

Had I thought about it, the story of the Prodigal Son would have been useful to communicate God's forgiving love. I could have stressed that the story is more about the father's love than the son's repentance. I probably also would have needed to explain that God does expect repentance and a desire to draw near to him as was evident in the Prodigal Son's experience. We often will receive insights as to how better to use the storying methods as we reflect on the experiences we have.

A Man on the Brink of Eternity

One Sunday afternoon I was asked to visit a man who was critically ill. He lived only a few blocks from the place where we were starting a new church yet, I had never seen him before.

When I got to his home, a woman, who turned out to be the man's daughter, met me at the door and guided me to a room where her father was in bed and breathing with a great deal of difficulty. After introducing myself, I told him that I had come to pray for him. He nodded approvingly and made a great effort to listen to what I was saying.

Because I sensed that he was in a lot of pain and was having difficulty hearing me, I decided to talk to him as simply as I could about the importance of our repenting of our sins and receiving Jesus as our Savior in order to be ready to meet our maker. I then asked him if he wanted to receive Jesus into his heart. To my astonishment he said "no." Sensing that he was near death I earnestly asked him why not. He answered: "I don't understand what you are telling me."

This sent chills down my spine realizing that this man was on the verge of dying. I then breathed a silent prayer asking God to help me to explain the way of salvation to this man. I then looked at the wall and saw a crucifix hanging right above the man's head. I took the crucifix and put it in front of him, pointed to Jesus and asked him: "Do you know who this is?"

"Yes," he answered "it is Jesus dying on the cross."

I then asked him: "Do you know why he is dying on the cross?"

"Yes," he replied "to teach us how to die."

I then answered and told him that it is true that Jesus died an exemplary death but that he came to show us how to live in this world and in heaven with him. This paved the way for me to tell him as briefly and simply as I could the story of the birth, life, death, and resurrection of Jesus. I explained that because of this if we repent of our sins and put our faith in Jesus we can receive eternal life and go to heaven when we die. I then prayed silently again and asked him: "Now do you understand why Jesus came and will you invite him to come into your heart to save you and give you eternal life?"

Without hesitation he said: "Yes, I want to invite Jesus into my heart."

I then asked him to repeat a brief payer after me. Very slowly yet firmly he prayed the prayer with me.

After praying for him and for his family, I left his home and began preparing for the evening service. That night the lady sent word that her father had gone to be with Jesus. I then thanked the Lord for giving me the privilege of visiting this man who was so close to eternity and for giving me the wisdom to use the crucifix as an objective lesson to tell this man the story of Jesus.

In this instance, I did not have the opportunity of hearing this man's story. Based on this man's cultural and religious background I could pretty well have guessed that he was an humble and poor man who had very limited formal education and who had very likely grown up with a very limited knowledge about God and Jesus, yet had never fully heard the story of Jesus.

His respect for religious objects was very evident in the sense of devotion he had for the crucifix. The crucifix, therefore, provided a bridge from the very limited and even distorted knowledge he had about Jesus to the story of salvation in Jesus Christ. There are times when objects, paintings, songs, and poems can provide these bridges as was true of the apostle Paul when he used the altar to the "unknown god" as a bridge to communicate the gospel of salvation to the people in the city of Athens.

Observations

First, I did not attach a date to each of these accounts of the experiences I have related. Some of these occurred before I had a notion about the *LifeStory Encounter* approach, others when I was first starting to employ it, and still others took place after I had acquired more experience. Please refrain from seeing these as "perfect examples" of the manner in which we can employ this type of storying. Instead, see them as a part of my learning experience.

Thinking back on some of these instances I know that I could have done a better job of listening or sharing. I am still learning and each experience is a new and exciting challenge. Our goal, therefore, is not to "develop a perfect method that is followed laboriously" but to respond to people in the various situations of life and to permit the Lord to speak through us.

Second, initially my goal was to get to the Story of Jesus as quickly as possible. As time has gone on, I have learned that in some instances it may be necessary to tell other Bible stories before getting to The Story. In the case with the young lady with a Muslim background, during the course of our conversation she said that she had heard that Jesus had treated a sinful woman (Mary Magdalene) with dignity and gentleness. Since she brought it up, it would have been insensitive of me not to pick up on that. It provided a bridge for us to continue to talk about Mary Magdalene and to begin to focus on the forgiveness that Jesus offers repented sinners.

Third, I am much more open now to selecting a Bible story (e.g., The Prodigal Son) as a bridge to The Story (of Jesus). The aim, obviously, would not be to share a bridging story just for the sake of doing so. There are instances, however, in which a bridging story fits the situation exactly and enables the unsaved person to identify with the character of the story in such as way as to create a high degree of interest and openness. That is the reason why we have suggested some "bridging stories" in the previous chapter.

Fourth, as you think of the various themes that might come up as people share their personal stories you may want to think of particular stories that might provide a bridge to The Story of Jesus. This reflection, however, takes time and thought. I find it helpful to try to link stories with themes ahead of time. For example, if the theme is one of joy and celebration, the story of Jesus at the wedding at Cana of Galilee or the account of Jesus having a meal at the home of Mary and Martha would serve as an effective bridge. Linking stories with themes can help us to be prepared so that when we are conversing with someone we can listen to them attentively instead of worrying about what story we need to share.

Fifth, please be aware that this is a dynamic process. You may use one bridging story in one instance and a totally different one in another occasion even if the themes are similar. It is important to have several bridging stories fresh in your mind and to be sensitive to the leading of the Holy Spirit.

Sixth, please keep in mind that the experiences we have shared with you do not represent a complete list of the themes that can be addressed in the *LifeStory Encounter* approach. These are simply examples of situations that we have encountered. There are many more themes that people might bring up and many more situations in which they find themselves. We are confident that there are enough stories in the Bible to enable us to share the good news of salvation with people in every situation of life.

I personally view the Gospel of Jesus Christ as a multifaceted diamond that has a word of hope for every person in the world. If people are looking for a sense of peace, release from a feeling of guilt, hope for the future, unconditional love, a sense of purpose, strength to face the challenges of life, assurance about life after death, or whatever spiritual yearning they might have in their hearts, they will find it in Jesus. It could be that one of these promises from God will be their overwhelming present need that brings them to Christ.

Once they do turn to Christ in faith they will find as the apostle Paul says that: "My God shall supply your every need according to his riches in glory in Christ Jesus" (Phil 4:19). Focusing on that particular initial need and finding the best story that provides the bridge can be the instrument that enables them to have a personal experience of salvation in Jesus Christ.

Seventh, the themes that we have discussed are simply examples of the types of themes that people will focus on during their conversations. Even though these may be some of the major themes that people talk about, there are many others that will surface in conversation. In addition to the themes of Joys and Achievements, Life-shaping Influences, Sorrows and Difficulties, and Changes and Challenges that we mentioned in chapter one, other themes surfaced in chapter two. Some of these were: A Search for Purpose in Life, A Strong Sense of Guilt, Overwhelming Problems, Need for Forgiveness, and Concern about Eternity.

Eighth, some of the conversations that arise as we relate to people will center on the peoples' own felt needs. Steve Douglass, the new Executive Director of Campus Crusade, stresses the importance of focusing on felt needs while witnessing to people. He explains:

> By starting your talk with a felt need, you establish rapport with your audience, preparing them for the spiritual portion of your presentation. Your goal is to transition to your spiritual topic naturally. As you build on their felt need, the transition works well because it allows your audience to warm up to your message. It should then be much easier to move from a felt need to the real need at the core – the need for Jesus Christ.[16]

The stories that Douglass suggests are actually the personal testimonies that Christians share with groups of unbelievers. He believes that these testimonies can be arranged around a "motivational" theme. Douglass has arranged his presentation around five categories of deeper felt needs:

- Group 1: Peace, Satisfaction, Freedom from Anxiety;

- Group 2: Significance, Success, Ultimate Purpose in Life;
- Group 3: Love Friendship, Freedom from Loneliness;
- Group 4: Security, Forgiveness, Sense of Well-Being;
- Group 5: Joy, Happiness, Enjoying Life.[17]

Under each of these categories, Douglass suggests questions that can be asked to engage people in conversation.

Ninth, as you can see, because the life experiences of people are so varied, there are many themes or deeper felt needs upon which people focus when they share their stories. The more preparation we can make in advance, the more effective we will be in connecting with the stories of people and moving naturally to the place where they hear The Story with interest and receptivity.

This process should never become a mechanical exercise in which we automatically pull up a story for each felt need. We must depend on the guidance of the Holy Spirit. Being aware of the possible themes that might surface and the Bible stories we might share will be very helpful. Remember that we are admonished in Scripture to "always be ready to give an answer of the hope that is in us" (1 Peter 3:15).

Tenth, we want to emphasize once again that LifeStory Encounters can be the starting point for involving people in long-term Bible Storying that focuses on discipleship, church starting, and leadership training. We see *LifeStory Encounters* as only the starting point.

Eleventh, LifeStory Encounters often take place with regard to people whom we may never see again. As was the case with Philip and the Ethiopian man, at times we are unexpectedly presented with God-ordained appointments. We should never underestimate these. Therefore, we should be prepared and be sensitive to the Holy Spirit for the time when he says "draw near to that person."

Twelfth, our hope and prayer is that *LifeStory Encounters* helps you to understand that there are numerous ways in which Bible Storying can take place. In his book *Basic Bible Storying*, J.O. Terry suggests that Bible stories can be used to prepare persons to view the *JESUS Film*, in hospital visits, in connection with ministry projects (medical, eyeglass, and dental clinics), in connection with relief efforts (earthquakes, storms, tsunamis), celebrations (births, weddings, anniversaries), literacy projects, English as a Second Language, and a wide variety of other settings.[18]

Thirteenth, the ideal is for Bible Storying to take place with a group over an extended period of time. That is not an option when we are unexpectedly presented with the opportunity of sharing the good news of salvation with a total stranger. It is wonderful, therefore, to have a "plan B" and to move right on with it to lead people to Christ in a wide variety of situations.

As we have stated before, part of the preparation involves the process of reviewing our own stories and those of others close to us. That is exactly what J.O. Terry is going to do in the following chapters.

CHAPTER 3

PERSONAL LIFESTORIES

J.O. Terry

As has been suggested, Bible storying begins with the story of the storyer. The experiences of the ones telling the stories point the way for sharing The Story, that is, the story of Christ. Certainly, the story of the one telling his/her story never replaces the Bible stories. These stories simply prepare the way for the stories from the Bible, help establish relationships for communication, and direct focus to the main story of Christ.

The stories of the Storyers pave the way for opportunities to share the Story of Christ in personal encounters. I will, therefore, begin with my story.

My Story

The Beginning of My Story

I was born and lived the first nine years of my life in my grandmother's home in a small town in southwestern Louisiana. Much of this time was during the World War II years. We had a large floor model radio in a wood cabinet that the family gathered around to listen to favorite programs each evening. There was no television and homes did not have air conditioning in those days. In the summertime the house was warm and stuffy, especially in the evenings. Houses then had large front porches or galleries which served as a gathering place for family members who stepped outside to catch a breath of fresh air.

On really warm nights my whole family moved out onto the porch or into the small front lawn right on busy U.S. 171. We had those tubular steel lawn chairs that were easy to drag off the porch to the lawn. What did we do? Or should I say what did the adults do? They told stories. And that experience of listening to stories is the beginning of my story.

In those days apparently no one was concerned about children staying up late, so we stayed with the adults until the house cooled off enough so we could go inside and go to bed. I don't remember any of those stories, but I can still vividly picture the scene of the adults sitting around in the dark talking, sharing their experiences, stories about what they had done or that had happened to them or others they knew. This was at my dad's home.

About twenty miles east of town my mother's folks lived on a farm with no electricity, a well with rope and bucket, and toilet out near the barn. They did not stay up as late as things got pretty dark after sunset. After eating supper sitting at a table lit by a kerosene lamp, my grandparents and uncle, when he was there, would repair to the front porch to take "a breath of air" before turning in for the night.

These front porch sittings seldom lasted more than an hour and ended around eight p. m. No one said much in the dark. My grandfather smoked a pipe. My uncle rolled his own cigarettes from his cloth bag of tobacco and papers. He would hunker on the front edge of the porch and stare off into the night. When anyone said anything, his usual response was only one or two syllables at most. It would be, "Yep" or "Uh huh." Then silence. Not much story there.

But at times I could get my grandparents to share some of their stories, like when the branch rose and flooded their garden, or when a large buck deer jumped the garden fence and ate the vegetables. Another story was about the time the stove flue pipe had a fire in it and it roared up the flue so that sparks set the cypress shingle roof on fire.

The real action, however, came when someone turned off the

gravel road and drove up in front of the house. My grandparents would shout to them, "Get out and come up!" (The house sat on cypress blocks about three feet off the ground.) Then the stories would fly about so and so who did such and such, or who ran away with a soldier, or whose old cow died.

Most of the stories were the usual accounts of experiences but they were interesting and animated. After a steaming cup of coffee on even the hottest July or August afternoon, and the sharing of all the news that was fit to share, the guest would leave. On lucky days whatever news they had left would provoke continuing discussion for awhile.

There was not much that I could say so I developed the art of listening. The highest form of the art is to listen while pretending not to be listening, or doing something else so as not to give ones self away. Some of their stories left me with plenty of questions to sort out later.

A few choice stories were especially memorable. One that I have particularly remembered is because it relates to some of the pre-story activity we often do in Bible Storying. The story went something like this:

Making Old George Thirsty

My grandfather had an old black horse named George. He wasn't a very large horse and probably was very old at the time. During most of the year, George just stayed in his stall and waited for his dipper of oats every morning, and occasionally came out for a drink in a large rusty iron tub that had been used to boil sugar cane juice in earlier years. But when springtime came, and it was time to break up the sod and plow the field to get ready for planting, it was George's time to work.

The field was several hundred yards away from the barnyard and there was no water up there. The days were getting warm by then and the plowing would be hard work. My grandfather wanted

George to drink water, but George hadn't been doing anything all night to make him thirsty.

You know that old saying about taking a horse to water, but you can't make him drink. Well, you can make him drink if you know how. Cleverly my grandfather would sprinkle some salt in George's ration of oats and feed him. It wasn't long before George would saunter out of his stable over to the water pot and drink up.

Then watered and ready to go, he would be hitched to the sled that carried the plow to the field. And there George would earn his keep. George stayed up there all day. He got to rest under a large pecan tree while we had lunch and the obligatory afternoon nap on a feather bed in the sweltering afternoon heat. Then we returned to the field and George would pull that plow for another hour or two before finishing for the day.

Perhaps you are wondering how this story relates to Bible Storying. One of the purposes of the pre-story dialogue time is to stir up interest in the theme or topic of the soon-to-be-told story. So a clever Bible storyer will ask some rhetorical questions to stir up interest and to raise questions that the Bible story will address. So we say that it is good to give your listeners a little "salt" to make them thirsty to hear the story. George expired a few years later but he lives on in this story.

My story must now turn back to town and my dad's family place. During those years while my dad was away in the war and later while he worked in another city during the week, we lived with his mother. In those days one lit the burners on the stove with strike-anywhere matches that came in those large red and white boxes. So there was always a box on the cabinet counter near the stove.

Well, this five year-old boy was fascinated with matches and just loved to strike them and watch them burn down to an ember. Then he would blow them out at the last moment. The adults were fussy about children playing with fire and I had been warned about playing with matches. But in unsupervised moments I always seized the opportunity to strike a few. I considered playing with the matches and the fire to be most entertaining. On one of those occasions the following event happened.

A Word to the Wise

During those days an older unmarried uncle also lived in the same house with us. He worked at the nearby post office. He usually came home for lunch and sometimes would just take off from work and come by the house. I was unsupervised at the moment and attracted to the box of matches within easy reach. It was just my luck that about the time I struck a match, I heard his footsteps coming up the back steps and through the porch door. I quickly blew the match out and fanned the air to disperse the evidence. My uncle stepped through the kitchen door just as I hid the still smoking match behind my back. He did not say a word about what was all too evident I had been doing.

Instead, he disarmed me by asking if I would like to hear a story. Whew! I thought, he isn't going to say anything. And besides, he was always telling stories about this thing or that place. When I got older, I realized that his stories mostly came from Readers' Digest! So he sat in the living room and I climbed into his lap as I had done many times before. His story went something like this:

Once upon a time there was a boy about your age. He looked a lot like you. He lived in a big house with his family. There were many things he liked to do, but one thing he really liked to do was to strike matches and watch them burn. This should have been a clue that the story was going to take an ominous turn! He would strike a match and watch it burn. Then just before the flame reached his fingers, he would quickly blow it out. When it stopped smoking he put it down and struck another one.

It seems the boy had been doing this one afternoon while he was home alone. After supper that night the boy took a bath and got ready for bed. He looked in the mirror as he brushed his teeth and combed his hair. He smiled at the face looking back at him, turned out the light and went to bed.

The next morning when the boy woke up he went to the bathroom to wash the sleep out of his eyes. He splashed some water on his face and looked in the mirror as he dried his face and hands. His ear was missing! The boy put his hand to his head where there used to be an ear. But there was none. He blinked and looked again; it was still missing.

"This is very strange," the boy thought to himself. "Last night before I went to bed, I had two ears. Now I have only one. I must be dreaming. Soon I will wake up and find that I still really have two ears." So he got dressed and soon forgot all about his missing ear. He could still hear out of the other one. And when he got a chance, and no one was looking, he struck several matches and watched them burn.

After supper and a bath the boy looked in the mirror. The ear was still missing. But everything else was still in place. "Tomorrow," he thought, "when I wake up the dream will be ended and I'll have two ears." And with that he went to bed and was soon sound asleep.

Early the next morning, as soon as the boy woke up, he hurried into the bathroom to look into the mirror. Horrors! Not only was his ear missing, now an eye was missing! "This dream is too much," he thought. "I know it will soon end and I'll have two ears and two eyes." But he could still see out of the remaining eye so the boy soon forgot all about his missing eye.

And again he played with matches and enjoyed watching the flame slowly burn down the matches. After supper the boy carefully studied his face. The ear was still missing. The eye was still missing. "Tomorrow the dream will end." So he went to bed.

The next morning the boy jumped out of bed and ran to the bathroom to look in the mirror. Oh no! The ear was still missing. The eye was still missing. And now his nose was gone as well!

At this point my uncle ended the story, put me down, got up and went his way. That is an eerie feeling after a story like that. I found myself feeling of my ears and my eyes and nose. I was thinking how lucky I was to have both my ears and both my eyes and still have a nose. I thought to myself, "It would be good to stop playing with matches before something bad happens to me like happened to that boy."

Characteristics of Stories

The accounts of my story reveal certain characteristics of stories in general. Stories have the power to provide vast amounts of information, advice, warning, inspiration, and emotion. Stories can many times actually communicate when other methods have failed. Note the characteristics of stories.

Stories are Powerful

The story above happened when I was around five, over sixty-five years ago. It hasn't faded from my memory. It lingers in the background when I light my barbecue grill! I have shared this story because it illustrates how powerful stories are when told in such a way that a person can relate to the story. My uncle never mentioned seeing me strike the matches, though I now suspect that he knew.

My dad would have whipped me with his belt if he had been there. That was his style of warning and doling out justice. But I was a hard-headed adventurous kid who quickly got over a thrashing and returned to whatever it was I had been punished for. But a story! It came in under my radar. I could see the story happening as my uncle told it. I saw that boy and his missing ear, eye, and nose. It was vivid. When my uncle put me down, I was jolted back into reality. But the story stuck.

It would be many years later before I saw firsthand how powerful Bible stories were to warn, instruct, and to bring people to faith in Jesus. But I also learned along the way that listeners who heard the Bible stories about things that related to their lives, not only believed the stories to be true, but they believed that if those things could happen back in those days, they could happen again today.

Stories Elicit Responses

A fellow missionary, working in a South American country, told of a listener's words after hearing the Old Testament stories about sin and God's judgment. The person said, "If those stories are true, then we are fried!"

There have been numerous stories about how listeners heard a Bible story and their lives were changed. Many of these stories reveal how stories often are the openings for people to respond to the message of Christ. One story comes from former missionary John Witte who then served in Kenya and nearby countries. John told a story of a miraculous conception.

The Story of Joseph and Martha Makrer

As I walked five kilometers to church in the African country of Sudan on Sunday April 30, 2001, with Bernardo, we met a couple who was plowing with oxen. They invited me to plow with them. I joined them. From there begins the story of one of the greatest ministry experiences I have ever had. I plowed a row that was laughable at best. Believe me, everyone was laughing. But it was probably my one opportunity to use an ox plow. Bernardo and I went on to church and had a great time that day.

The next day after doing devotions at our clinic, I was riding in the back of our pickup truck together with a new Christian named Samuel Magwor. Samuel is also our radio operator and we call him "Sierra Mike," his radio name. As we went along there were some guys working on the road, cutting down trees and filling last year's ruts with the logs, in preparation for the rains.

One of the guys in that work crew waved and yelled out to

Sierra Mike, "That white man (*kawaja*) plowed my field yesterday." We waved and went on. Later, I said to Sierra Mike, that we should go visit the man later that day. It seemed odd to me that I should see him again. So at the end of the day we went.

Sierra Mike and I walked for 45 minutes to get to Joseph's house. On the way I was wondering what I might say to Joseph. I thought I might tell the parable of the soils again since I had met him plowing. But on the way Sierra Mike told me, "I know this guy and I know what his problem is." It turns out Joseph had been married to Martha his wife for five years without being able to have a baby.

Childlessness is a really a major problem in Dinka culture. Martha is a pretty lady and it is likely that Joseph paid upwards of one-hundred head of cattle for her. With such a large dowry comes the pressure to produce. She had not given him a child. Sierra Mike also told me that Joseph was so desperate to have a child that he was even selling his cattle to raise money to take Martha to Uganda for fertility treatments.

I now knew how serious the problem really was, because Dinka simply do not sell their cattle! I thought about Abraham and Sarah's story and, being committed to storying, I knew what I would say to Joseph and Martha. Along the way people were calling out to Sierra Mike asking him if that was the white man they saw plowing the day before in the yellow shirt. They asked where we were going and Sierra Mike told them. Everyone knew we were going to visit the Makrers.

When we finally arrived, Joseph was a little surprised. He walked us into his compound and we sat down on a couple of logs. After exchanging pleasantries he leaned over to me and said, "I am just an ordinary Dinka man, what are you doing at my house?" He had seen plenty of white men, but they always went to see the dignitaries of the community.

I told him I wasn't sure, but I had met him the day before and again this morning. He broke in and said, "Yesterday was Sunday wasn't it. Maybe God meant for us to meet." I agreed and asked if Martha was around. She wasn't, she had gone to the well to get water. So we said we'd like to wait for Martha.

After just a few minutes Joseph asked me the next obvious African question, "Do you have a family?" I took this as an opportunity. I told him all about my wife and FOUR CHILDREN, and particularly all about Ben, and how special it was to have a son. I knew this was killing him inside. But I was setting him up. Then I asked him the same question, "Do you have children?"

He said very dejectedly, "No, but I've taken a second wife who lives in the cattle camp, and we've had two girls. And I'll tell you a secret. I have five illegitimate daughters in this community." The guy was so desperate he was sleeping with women all over the community, but was only making girls! I couldn't wait to tell him Abraham's story. I also took the opportunity to teach him that the sex of the baby is determined by the man. So his quest for a son was not only Martha's problem, it was his also.

When Martha arrived she came over to sit down and we began. We told her we had come to encourage them by sharing the word of God with them concerning their barrenness. For the next forty minutes I told them the entire story of Abraham and Sarah. They were completely in tune with the story. They laughed where they should have laughed. They were surprised when they should have been. This story sounded so much like their own personal story.

When we finished we prayed for them to have a baby and encouraged them to trust in God. But I never in any way tried to share the Gospel directly with them. I had no sense that the Holy Spirit was leading me to do that. I only mentioned the name of Jesus as I closed the prayer for them in his name.

As we left, Joseph walked with us up to a certain tree. From there Sierra Mike could find our way home. On the way Joseph and

Sierra Mike talked. Joseph told him, "I don't even care if my wife has a baby now. I just consider it a miracle that you came to my house. I have such a peace in my heart." I wondered about that. I know that a lost man can only experience that kind of peace if God gives it to him. But I had not even shared a clear gospel witness. What could he mean?

After Joseph left us Sierra Mike and I talked about the encounter. I said, "Can you imagine what would happen if Martha got pregnant with a baby boy." Sierra Mike said, "If that happens, this whole community will believe in Jesus."

As I traveled to the States in the month of June, speaking in various churches, everywhere I told this story, and asked people to pray for Joseph and Martha Makrer. We prayed specifically that Martha would conceive and have a baby boy. I rarely ask people to do this kind of thing. But this time I felt impressed by the LORD to lead people to pray this way. Everyone kept saying, be sure and let us know what happens.

On July 24, 2001, Sierra Mike called me on the radio. He was so excited. The first thing out of his mouth was "Praise the Lord!" which is not appropriate radio protocol, particularly in Southern Sudan. He said, "John, I have just come from your friend's house, and I want to give a partial report. The woman you prayed for is pregnant. She just came from our clinic and they say she has been pregnant for almost three months." As I began to look at the calendar, I realized it had been almost three months exactly since we visited them and first prayed for them![19]

God Will Somehow Save Isaac

Bible stories affect listeners in other ways. In the "EE-TAOW!" video, Mark Zook told the story of Abraham and how God had asked him to sacrifice his son, his only son, Isaac. Mark told the story up to the point of the sacrifice and stopped for the day. Mark recorded his teaching so a cassette tape was available for review on a hand-cranked cassette player. One older man listened to the story again on tape. Then he went to Mark to tell him that he just knew that God was somehow going to save Isaac.[20]

That Story Bothered Us

I have had the experience of telling one of the Bible stories and having listeners unwilling to discuss the story immediately after hearing it. These same people, however, would come the following week and say , "That story you told us last week bothered us. We have been thinking about it all week."

Then they were ready to talk. The listeners needed time to process the story and so it stayed active on their heart until we met again. The chance to discuss the story came after a time.

Tell Me Again About My Name

LaNette Thompson recalled the time in Burkina Faso when she told the story of Adam and Eve to a group of women. One of the women had the name "Hawa" which is similar to the Hebrew for Eve. Here is LaNette's account:

> After talking for awhile, one woman looked directly at LaNette and said, "My name is *Hawa*. What is yours?" LaNette was shocked because exchange of name was so rare. She gave her name which all the women repeated several times. When each woman was introduced, LaNette said it would be difficult to remember all their names. The women laughed and said, "Bring a paper and write down our names and you will remember." LaNette told the woman named *Hawa* that her name was the same as that given to the first woman that God created. Later *Hawa* touched LaNette's arm and said, "Tell me again about my name." The women were open to learning.[21]

Do You Know Your Own Personal Story?

When my wife and I applied for appointment as missionaries one of the requirements for candidates was to write a synopsis of their LifeStories allowing one page for each year of their life. At the time I was 32 and so my target was 32 pages. My wife is somewhat more methodical than I so she set about outlining her life year by year. I sat and thought stretching my memory back as far as I could.

We were able to include several events and experiences in our writing. We were to tell about our family, our spiritual journey to salvation and discipling, and especially to recall how we saw God's hand in directing our lives to a call to serve Him as missionaries.

After sitting at a typewriter for some time, I began to see the story and as it unfolded. After getting off to such a slow start I'll confess that I was hard-pressed later on to limit my personal story to just 32 pages. It included a brief account of how God spared my life when I was helping a friend to run some electric wires under his house.

I was lying in rainwater that had collected in the area under the house. That is an amazing experience when a terrific shock hits you like that and you know this is it—you are going to die and then nothing. A short time later with a loud buzzing my ears, my heart beat over 200, an adrenaline rush that is beyond comprehension, I realized that I was still alive as consciousness returned like that proverbial rushing out of a tunnel into the daylight.

Obviously, I survived and after a few days of complete rest to let my heart rate settle, I was back to work. Two things were evident to me afterward. One is that my life truly was in God's hands and He could take it any time He so chose. A second evident matter was that God must have some work for me to do and so He preserved my life at a time when I would have certainly died.

As I reflected over our first years of married life I remembered how little money we had lived on. In spite of limited finances, we still had three healthy children. I realized that somehow God would provide for our needs in the coming years.

The story I continued to write told of our sudden feeling of a call to move to Fort Worth instead of attending seminary in nearby New Orleans. The only work I could find in Fort Worth paid $75 a week but it was enough. I had enrolled in Southwestern Baptist Theological Seminary. One Sunday after our pastor returned from an evangelism crusade in the Far East, he preached on his experiences while there. My wife and I felt called to surrender for missions.

That morning the personnel officer for the Baptist Radio and Television ministry was among those who came by to speak. He asked me to come see him the next day about the very job that I had hoped to get when we first moved to Fort Worth. But then my heart sank. I had just committed myself to missions, how could I take the job? After praying about the matter, the Lord seemed to direct me to take the job.

To make a long story short, that job soon put me in touch with missionaries who were using radio broadcasting in their ministries. I was "borrowed" by the then Baptist Foreign Mission Board to go to a number of countries to train local workers and help to establish radio recording studios. And while on one of those trips to Guatemala the missionary I was helping said that God had led him to speak with me about seeking appointment as a missionary.

When I returned home my heart was heavy again as we had bought a house, replaced all our early marriage furniture, and I loved the job I had. But God was still at work and while I was away. He had also spoken to my wife about the need to fulfill our commitment to seek appointment as missionaries.

All of these and many other experiences have contributed to my LifeStory. I could now clearly understand that all along God was working out what I was going to do. I will add in just one story along that line.

My dad was stationed in the Philippines during World War II, going in with the army engineers when the country was retaken from the Japanese. He brought back many photographs of old Manila and told of his experiences while stationed there. I didn't know it then but a seed had been planted. In my work with the radio ministry I was asked by a missionary who served in the Philippines to help him acquire a certain piece of recording equipment and ship it to him. This established a relationship.

Two years later he asked if I could visit Manila while on a trip to that area. I did and consulted on the new recording studio soon to be built. Then when my wife and I applied for missionary appointment you will never guess where it was recommended that I serve! So we were appointed for the Philippines.

We were not spared from one of the challenges of living in that part of the world. Only two years into our service our house was partially destroyed in a very powerful typhoon. I wasn't even in the country at the time so my family endured and came through it alone. God was gracious to us during those years. Our children had good school experiences. We remained healthy and I loved the radio ministry and had a wonderful experience working under an older missionary as we complemented each other in the radio ministry there.

I'll not elaborate on any more of these stories. The point is that I came to realize that I had a wealth of personal stories that dated back to my early years and continued on through my marriage, our move to Fort Worth, and final move to the Philippines. But there was one question that had never been adequately answered all those years—Why me? I had a younger brother. Why did God pick me and not him?

The answer came only recently during the days before my mother died at 95 after outliving my dad by 30 years. One night while she was in the hospital, the week before she died, she talked all night long. As my mother relived her life I learned many things about the time she left her parents on the farm and moved to town, how she met my dad, and their marriage and coming to live at my grandmother's house. And during one of the many times she reflected on these things she said: "When you were born, I dedicated you to God!" There! That was the missing piece of my LifeStory! There was a definite beginning after all. I was just too young to know it.

I have belabored the reader with parts of my story. In doing so, I hope that I have planted the thought that you also have a LifeStory composed of many component stories. And if you will closely examine your own story you will certainly find God's hand at work there, too. We should not be envious of another's LifeStory for if we take the time to reflect on our lives, we will see a rich treasure of God's presence in our lives.

We Don't Live in Isolation

Unless you are a hermit or stranded on a desert island you live your LifeStory in the midst of other people who have their own LifeStories. You interact with their stories. And so your own personal LifeStory is mingled with and merged with others around you and so becomes part of "our story." Just as many LifeStories of those around me influenced my story, so it happens with all of us. Every reader should accept the fact that he/she has a LifeStory and that this story can be used by the Lord to communicate with other people. No one is devoid of a LifeStory.

One real disadvantage of my writing to you in a book is that we cannot exchange our stories. I am telling you part of mine but I cannot in turn hear your story. Writing is wonderful for preserving the content of our life stories. Face-to-face sharing exchanges, however, not only the content, the facts, but also the emotions we experience.

Our stories do not end as long as we draw a breath. Even as I write these lines I am preparing to return to a country where I traveled and worked for over twenty years among a people that I came to know and love. God has been so gracious to give me this gift of a return to that "story-land" where so many ministry stories happened and I heard so many stories from those I worked among.

Not all our LifeStories are alike. Some are exciting. Some are sad. Some are surprises as things happened we did not expect and perhaps turned out much better than we anticipated. Many of our stories may appear to us to be unique but we may find that others have had similar experiences. More on this later about the repeating patterns in our LifeStories.

Before continuing let me add a story or two about how I became involved in Bible Storying. These stories will indicate my own introduction to using stories in ministry. My background is in broadcasting with programming that told the stories of other people. Because of my experience in media, I was asked to help some of my mission organization's co-workers in using sets of Bible story lessons and Bible teaching pictures. My education and involvement began at this point.

My first meeting with pastors and evangelists to study the use of Bible story lessons was in Dhaka, Bangladesh. The effort was hardly a success. Due to my own lack of real knowledge and actual experience in using the story resources, my presentation was not met with very much enthusiasm. I realized that I needed to learn more before attempting any future conferences. So I traveled to the Philippines to sit at the feet of a Filipino chronological Bible story trainer. The experience of learning from him one-on-one for five days was both helpful and humbling. The training paid rich dividends as it gave me the overview that I needed to really begin learning.

Sometime later I was back in Bangladesh to take this new teaching out to the villages. My very first assignment sent me to a village where I was to teach all I knew about using the chronological Bible story teaching in one day. So equipped with a book of Bible story lessons and my Bible I arrived to find a group awaiting my teaching.

We entered the church building which was made of mud with a thatch roof. It had a rear door but no windows and no lights. It was dark inside. I was to teach the group facing the bright sunlight streaming in the door toward my eyes. I had my Bible in one hand and the book of story lessons in the other hand and could not see either one.

I had all day to teach! God was gracious and I was able to make it to the first mid-morning break when I rushed outside to quickly study ahead. Somehow I made it through the day covering some 35 Bible stories from Creation to the Ascension. What a relief when the day finally ended. But the story did not end there as I had another day of the same yet to come.

The following day my interpreter and I traveled to a different village. They also had a church building but decided to hold the teaching on a covered porch where there was daylight, precious wonderful daylight, so I could see my Bible and story book. But there was a new challenge. The roof was high enough for the short village people but just high enough for a six foot person to teach all day with his head bowed! It was interesting to find that I really did not need to refer to the story book or Bible much after the experience the day before. Later I felt the Lord had used these early experiences as a Bible story boot camp.

Later training conferences were five days long and I would be teaching up to seven hours a day. I quickly learned why my Filipino friend had so strongly encouraged me to develop a panorama of the Bible stories because this is what my listeners needed to see the larger picture before exploring the individual stories one-by-one and how they were related.

Within a year or so teaching these training conferences helped my own Bible story library to grow to around one hundred stories. By then I was holding my Bible in my hand when telling the stories as a signal this was the source of the stories, but I hardly needed to refer to the open Bible unless my interpreter needed a verse reference so he could refer to his own Bible.

In the evenings we shared our stories and as a practicum retold the Bible stories. Some of the most interesting stories I heard were about the dreams that some of the listeners had in which Jesus appeared to them. In every case that dream had been a life-changing experience for them. I asked how they knew it was Jesus. Some said they recognized him from the pictures they had seen. Others said they just knew it was Jesus. A few said that Jesus introduced himself. There was not as much persecution in those early days as people experience in this day. I am sure their stories now would tell of the fear and suffering that has since spread into some of their villages. The peak of the Bible story teaching was in the mid-1990's. As I write these words there is harvest where seeds were being sown.

To my delight I was able to make a return visit to South India where I had told the Bible stories at times to crowds of hundreds of people. I discovered that now my Indian brothers and sisters are telling the stories and teaching them to their house church members to empower them in turn to tell the stories to their neighbors and families. The story that God began in my life is now their story and in time will be the story of many in that land. Their LifeStories are their testimonies of what Christ has done in their lives and among their family members.

These accounts show the tremendous possibilities that exist as we share our LifeStories with others. We can lead them to share their LifeStories with us and with others in their networks. From these relationships, people can and will encounter the Story of Jesus. Then, these people who find Christ will share Him with others.

CHAPTER 4

THE VALUE OF UTILIZING LIFE STORIES

J.O. Terry

Trevor McIlwain, a pioneer in popularizing of chronological Bible teaching, spoke of the need for the Old Testament stories to prepare a people to receive and understand the Gospel stories. He was convinced that the Old Testament stories served to develop an awareness of God's righteousness, his judgment for sin, and the fact that man could not save himself from God's wrath. Without these stories as a prelude or backdrop for the Gospel, McIlwain taught that the Gospel story of salvation would be "sown into hard, unploughed, poorly prepared, thorny ground."[22] He was convinced that one must present stories of the "bad news" as a backdrop for the "good news."

While this consideration is generally true for strategic chronological presentations, actual practice has found that many times people are already at the story of Jesus and that we should begin with this Story. In other ministry encounters many storyers have found that they need to select a story that is relevant to the immediate need and that provides answers for gaps in knowledge, encouragement, correction, or just comfort. So any relevant Old Testament or New Testament story could be the needed story for the ministry encounter.

The bad news stories are not, however, always needed as many people have for various reasons already come under a sense of God's judgment and their hopeless condition to change their situation. But for others the Old Testament stories do serve to give a perspective that is needed. The next section considers the relational aspect of stories. And as such, many listeners who hear the Old Testament stories relate to the stories because of things they have done or because of the moral, social, or spiritual condition of their people.

It is beyond the scope of this book to deal with which Old Testament stories should be employed and how many should be used. Consideration for selecting these Old Testament stories and other stories is explained further in the book, *Basic Bible Storying*. This section deals with the values inherent in utilizing Bible stories.

Stories are Relational

I am mentioning several characteristics of stories that are not mutually exclusive. For the purpose of illustration I am separating several of these characteristics. I hope that by doing this I can help the reader to see the power of personal stories that minister to a person and which can also be shared at a time and manner to inform and foster relationships.

These relationships develop first between the listener and the story or its characters or outcome, and then between the listener and Jesus as Savior. Relationships can be enhanced as stories are employed in the interactions between people.

Personal Stories Communicate

Stories are relational because they enhance the communication process between people. Perhaps, in that previous story from my life, you also saw the boy as he was losing his facial features. Stories can be very personal in this respect. To make these stories even more personal sometimes storyers will recast stories are used where the name, sex, place, or minor details of the plot or time of happening are changed to make the story more relational. It is still the same basic story but it is just adapted to make it more relational for listeners—to be like their experiences or to pose the possibility that the story could happen to them.

This technique has been helpful at times in getting a hearing by those who were resistant to anything "Christian" or foreign, or that in some other way were perceived as not applying to them as listeners. I have had personal stories fall flat as I shared them and the person listening did not relate to the story. Sometimes the listeners would simply dismiss the story, saying, "Well, that is your story. It has nothing to do with me."

Or, they might dismiss it with, "I'm not like that." Or, "Nothing like that ever happened to me." Listeners can make these judgments with pictures as well as stories. This happens because in some situations listeners cannot distance themselves from details in the stories that are unfamiliar or in some way counter to their experience or culture.

Let me illustrate this process. I used a favorite preaching poster many times while working in Asia. Preaching posters are large colorful flipcharts of several pages that tell a story. The ones I used were all developed for public witnessing by approaching the Gospel in different ways. This particular one was titled *The Village Pump*.[23]

The story is about a rusty pump in a village that gave smelly, dirty water. The villagers held a meeting to decide what needed to be done. First they decided the pump needed to be scraped and painted with a fresh coat of white paint. But the water was still smelly and dirty.

Then they decided that if someone gave a nice oration over the pump, it would be impressed and then give clean water. That didn't work either. A schoolteacher shared that when the boys in his class misbehaved and he thrashed them with a rod; that did the trick. So the teacher beat the pump until his rod broke. But that didn't work either.

Then the village medic suggested the problem was in the well and not with the pump. So he sent his son down into the well to clean out the debris and filth. Then the pump gave clean water.

The Bible teaching was about the heart and the sin that

needed confessing and cleaning out through faith in Jesus as Savior. In one place when I told that story, the people were very attentive to the story and obviously enjoyed hearing it. But when I began to talk about the implication of the story, the listeners dismissed the story saying, "Our pumps don't look like that!"

Limitations of Personal Stories

Stories do not always, however, lead to relationships. Some of the personal stories I used came from my experiences on my grandparents' farm. The rural listeners could both appreciate the stories and relate to them. When I spoke with students or people who lived in the cities, I used other stories that were more appropriate for them. But to be honest, there were many people and groups that I could not relate to easily by using my personal stories because my life had been so different even though I had lived in their part of the world for over three decades.

For them I used stories I had read or heard that I thought related in some manner. And after I had gained experience among the various peoples in my ministry network, I learned some of their stories that I heard and could use as well as stories of their heroes or historical figures from their recorded history.

Personal Stories Make Us Vulnerable

Another thing to consider in the use of personal stories is that our stories may make us vulnerable. I've already mentioned the possibility of our stories not being understood by listeners. There is also the possibility that stories can be misunderstood so that the listener is angered or rejects us and our story because of some unexpected outcome, or taking the story to mean something different than our reason for telling it.

Several accounts among the Bible stories involve a response to a story that included death. In 2 Samuel 1, a story speaks of a young man who came to David to tell the account of his role in

King Saul's death. The messenger's story was not well-received by David and actually led to the young man's demise.

A similar incident that involved death recorded the event when two men came to David to report their killing of King Saul's son, Absolom. They thought that David would be pleased to know that a potential rival claimant of the throne had been eliminated. Instead David was angry with their report and reminded the men of what happened in the previous story. David then had them put to death as well.

The story of Stephen in Acts also involves death. In Stephen's bold defense, he recounted the biblical story of the prophets leading up to Jesus. It stung the hearts of the religious leaders who were especially angered by how Stephen ended his testimony. The crowd responded by stoning Stephen to death.

When Peter and John were telling the story of Jesus, they were commanded by the religious authorities not to teach in the name of Jesus. But Peter and John replied, *"Judge for yourselves whether it is right in God's sight to obey you rather than God. For we cannot help speaking about what we have seen and heard"* (Acts 4:18-20).

A popular saying asks the question who will be the one "to tie the bell on the cat's neck?" But there are times when we must care enough to confront those we are listening to. And as Nathan did with David, he told a story that touched David's shepherd's heart and also related to the law of God that David surely knew. David was not angry with Nathan, but instead was convicted of his sin after realizing that the story was about him and what he had done. There are times when we must be bold to use stories that might possibly invoke the listener's wrath if we truly love and care for the listener.

In the early years of my missionary experience, I was delegated the task of speaking to an erring missionary who had a temper and was physically very strong. I opted to use a personal story to get his attention and bridge into talking about the error of his ways. I told a personal story. He listened to what I had to say and then laughed at me for "being so stupid."

He did not see the parallel to himself in the story and he rejected the story and ridiculed me as well. His ways did not mend and he later he had to leave the mission field. Looking back on that experience I realize that it may have been more prudent for several of us to confront him with the accusation rather than attempt to subtly and compassionately use a story to help him understand the error of his ways. Stories are often effective but those who use this method must realize that storying is not the only method.

Stories Can Be Misperceived

One of the factors we faced in sharing stories with oral communicators in rural places was that they sometimes could not distance themselves from pictures or even stories to see the embedded truths. Instead they were sometimes put off by the visual image and sometimes by things in the told stories because they could not find a way of relating to the story. Obviously, our choice of stories can be beneficial if our listeners can easily relate to them, and become a problem if they reject the story as "not like them" or outside their ability to perceive or understand.

Jesus understood well the culture of his day, but he, too, experienced times when even the disciples needed further explanation in order to understand the stories Jesus used in his teaching (See Mark 4:9-10). At other times when Jesus told stories to those gathered around him the Pharisees overheard the stories and knew the stories applied to them (See Matthew 21:45). We do not have records of any personal stories of his earlier years that Jesus may have used. The Gospel writers focused on the teaching stories and the stories of Jesus' public ministry.

We do know that early in his ministry Jesus had returned to Nazareth. When he was asked to teach in the synagogue, he told two Old Testament stories about foreigners that God helped when there was need. Obviously, Jesus used stories to impress His message on people.

The second story about Naaman the leper was especially galling to his listeners as it implied that though there were many lepers in the land of Israel that God cleansed only Naaman the Syrian. Partly because of this true story, Jesus was rejected by his own people and driven from the synagogue when the people tried to kill him. The one delivering such stories should seek to understand the meaning the story will have for the listeners.

Trust in Telling and Hearing Stories

Sometimes those we work with, if they do not know us well, may not trust us with their stories. Personal stories are kept close until a person feels confident that the story can be shared with a sympathetic person. I have worked with nationals in several countries where I commuted in and out over a period of time, seeing them fairly often as we worked together in radio listener follow-up or probing for potential response to the Gospel through Bible Storying rallies.

One of the significant contributions to an effective Bible story set for a group of listeners is to know the spiritual and cultural worldviews of the groups. This understanding helps us select the best stories to tell, guides us as to how best to tell the stories, alerts us to notice if there are things in the stories difficult to understand, or make sense of, and empowers us to foster the listeners' ability to relate and respond to the stories. So we gather as much information from potential listeners as possible to help us inform our choices of Bible stories and how to teach them.

Sometimes people who don't know us very well may be suspicious of our motives. Because we are outsiders, they do not share their insider stories. I have found that many times it would take two or three years of meeting and working together before the people came to trust me and be willing to share their stories with me.

A man in Bangalore that I worked with for over fifteen years only began to share personal stories after he felt that he could trust me and that I might still like him even after he told his stories. Following is one such story.

Mega's Story

One of the men in India who often served as my driver was the only believer in his Hindu family. God gave Mega a godly Christian wife. His parents expected the new wife to serve their Hindu gods which she would not do. The young man poured out his heart to me, concerned about being a good son to his parents and at the same time a good husband who honored and protected his Christian wife. We prayed for his parents and for him and his wife to be strong, forgiving, and loving toward the parents, but remaining true to following Jesus.

After the birth of two boys the wife became pregnant again, and fearing they could not afford to support and educate three children, she had an abortion. Mega was devastated. Finally he trusted me enough to tell what was on his heart. He talked as I listened and then we prayed. He had feared being under God's curse because of what his wife had done.

Later God gave them a beautiful daughter. Over those years we worked together he felt free to share many of his LifeStories with me. In turn as part of my training for him I shared appropriate LifeStories of my own in exchange. Often in such exchanges of stories, the Lord is able to enter the relationships and find entrance into the hearts of people.

A Story of Failure and Shame

While visiting Bangalore for following up on radio program listeners, I had some time at the mission office. Pastors and church planters would drop by to visit or to borrow books from the reference library. Sometimes the younger men would drop by just to talk. One afternoon a young evangelist came by. He seemed to be quite agitated. It was tea time so I invited him to sit outside in a covered area so we could enjoy our tea and talk freely.

The young man began to tell a story about his shame and failure. He had returned to a village where he had previously lived before he became a believer. There he shared about Jesus to some of his village gang. But they laughed at him and ridiculed him, beat him, and robbed him. They told him that if he ever came back they would kill him. So he left in humiliation and shame. He was hurting from the experience and ashamed of his failure.

When he finished his story I asked the names of those who had mistreated him. Then I asked if in his heart he could forgive them just as Jesus forgave from the cross those who were crucifying him. He thought about it for a moment and decided that he could. We talked some about how God sees and knows our suffering and is powerful to redeem our failures. Then we prayed for those men by name asking God to forgive them and to open their hearts.

After we had prayed it was evident that the burden of the young man's heart was lifted. I told him, "Let's see how God handles this."

Later the young man told me that he heard that one of the men in the village had died, one had fallen off a hill and broken his leg, and a third had been driven out of the village. That wasn't what we prayed for but it appears that justice had been done. What blessed me most was the change in his spirits after the young evangelist had told his story and we had prayed about it. I did not have an appropriate story to tell. All I did was to listen and then remind him of Jesus' story.

The Bible Storyer who has personal encounters with others will not always experience the event of the people telling their stories of failure. In fact, it is a more typical characteristic of oral people living in rural places not to tell shame stories involving loss of face. We don't like to share a story that will be ridiculed or that will provoke a wrong or undesired response. So we hide those stories, sometimes out of shame, or because of the hurts we experience again when the stories are recalled. It is not unusual for a person to wonder in their heart, "What will my friend think of me if I tell him/her my story?"

One of the men I worked with in India told me one day that "I had no face!" What he was saying was that when I failed I did not become ashamed and stop attempting to work. He was referring to problems he and others had when they failed in their work. Instead, he had noted that I simply tried again and kept trying until I accomplished my task. After my co-workers learned they could trust me to hear their stories, then they were free to tell their LifeStories that sometimes involved failure or what would bring shame in their culture.

I am not an aggressive interviewer because I tend to let a person tell their story, their way, without interrupting them. And I am loathe to press for yet untold details which they may or may not want to share out of respect for their privacy. I figure that if they want to tell me, they will.

I do not like to be interrupted when telling a story by some question that may or may not be relevant to the story as I am telling it. And the worst of all is for someone to jump in and summarily finish the story as they think it ought to end. So I prefer to listen and be patient and let a person tell their story, their way, with the details (extravagantly or sparsely) as they prefer.

I have a son who tells detailed stories. One needs patience as sometimes it is difficult to tell where the story is going and whether he is eventually going to get there or not. He usually does if you just leave him alone to finish his story. So it takes patience to be a good listener.

A characteristic I learned from my mother is to hear a story without interrupting or reacting to the story or to the one telling the story. She would simply hear the story. Sometimes she felt the need to comfort us after our stories or even to ask a question related to outcome or what we would need to do, but never to reject us for having told the story to her. We always felt a freedom to share our hearts with her even when we knew that she did not approve of something in the story.

Witnesses for Christ can help people have the freedom to share their stories by listening without reacting or questioning. This principle does not mean we accept sinful actions and words. It does mean that we try to enable people to tell their stories.

Personal Stories Can Teach Many Truths in One Story

There is a story that I have used at times to illustrate the consequences of sin. I have had to be careful in selecting the stories I share because I lived in a very different world than some of the people among whom I worked and shared my stories as they shared theirs.

Most of the listeners I shared this next story with knew about typewriters. They had seen them and had observed the user pressing the keys. I can only think of one time I used this story and the listeners politely accepted the story, but afterward I suspected that I could have been talking about a rocket to the moon and they wouldn't have understood that either! This story happened when I was the older brother and had a sister two years younger than me and a baby brother four years younger.

The Typewriter

My father had a small black Royal manual typewriter that he kept in a black case with a snap catch by the handle. He did not use the typewriter very much, but on occasion I had watched him open the case and raise the lid to reveal this marvelous machine with all those buttons that he pushed with his fingers. He would put in a piece of paper and turn that wheel on the side and the paper would miraculously go down into the machine and then come up again. It was wonderful.

When my father finished pushing those buttons, he would again turn that wheel on the side and the paper would come out. Then he slid the part that moved to the center and closed the lid and I heard the catch snap. Several times my father had said to me, "Don't touch." The marvelous machine was forbidden territory. The machine sat there in its black case day after day.

During those days my father worked in another city and would be gone during the week days. The machine sitting there all by itself bothered me. Each time I passed by the machine in the case was whispering, "Touch me!"

At last I could not stand the strain any longer. I knew how to open the case by sliding the catch aside. Surely it would not hurt anything at least to open the case and have a look. My father had said, "Don't touch." But he wasn't there, and I was only going to look. Certainly no harm could come from just doing that.

So I slid the catch and heard it click open. I raised the lid like I saw my father do many times. Wow! There it was that marvelous machine with all those buttons. I had already started school and knew my alphabet. "This is wonderful," I thought, "look at all those buttons with letters on them."

I decided to press one of the buttons to see what happened. I didn't have any paper, but I knew that when my father pushed the buttons something made a noise inside the machine.

So I pressed a button. The miracle happened as one of those things inside raised up with a clack and then fell back down. So I tried another one. It, too, rose up with a clack and fell back down. But somehow my father put all of his fingers on the buttons and pushed. So that must be what you do. So I put my fingers on as many buttons as I could and pushed. Many of those things inside came up, but this time they did not go back down.

I thought that maybe I needed to push another button so those would go down. But it came up and stuck, too. If I had quit here, things might have turned out better. But I decided to help the machine by pushing the things back down. Most went down but one or two of them bent and would not go down. I decided to close the case and maybe it would fix itself. So I closed the lid.

It was a week or two later when my father needed to type a letter. When I saw him going to the machine, I went into another room. I secretly hoped that he would not notice anything. He didn't even get his paper put into the machine before he called my name. Why me? I had a brother and sister and other adults were in the house from time to time.

When I came to him he asked, "Did you touch my typewriter?"

The words slipped out of my mouth as I looked around the room, "What typewriter?"

"You know very well what typewriter!" he said.

I thought to help him out by asking if he had checked with my sister (who couldn't reach the cabinet where the typewriter sat) and my baby brother who definitely couldn't reach it either. "No, I didn't touch your typewriter," I added.

Now the inquisition took a severe turn. "Did you touch my typewriter?"

"Well, I may have touched it, but that was all," I volunteered. I was beginning to wilt under this grueling questioning.

"Did you open the case? Did you push any of the keys? Why did you do this when I told you not to touch it!"

"I didn't do anything to it," I said, "is there something wrong?"

Again my father asked point blank, "Did you touch my typewriter?"

My father had developed x-ray vision before even Superman had it. His blue eyes could burn right into your soul. He wasn't saying anything, just looking straight at me.

Finally, I caved in. "I broke it, but I only meant to look at it."

My father's gaze continued for several more minutes. This was agony but I knew that even more agony was coming when he would take off his belt and administer small town justice. But he didn't.

"Okay," he began, "you lied to me. You did not tell me the truth. So you can't be trusted any more. And if you can't tell the truth, then you really should not be talking to anyone in the family. And they should not be talking to you. So for the next five days you will speak to no one. And I am telling your mother and grandmother not to speak to you, either."

Whew! I was feeling pretty good about getting off so light. The truth began to dawn on me when later I went to tell my mother something and she turned away from me. After this happened several times I realized that I had been exiled in my own house. My sister didn't help much by telling me that she wasn't supposed to talk to me. But that turned out to be hit or miss. When the adults gathered I was shunned. Now that hurt. It was a terrible week but it finally ended.

The typewriter was in the shop being repaired. My father called for me. "Now," he said, "I hope that you have learned your lesson. I was sad that you disobeyed me and broke my typewriter. But I was even sadder because you lied to me when I asked you to tell the truth. Do you think you can tell the truth from now on?"

I mumbled a feeble, "Yes, sir. I will always tell the truth from now on."

After another interminable staring session I was dismissed and things returned to normal. What a terrible experience being cut off from the family. I could see them but could not talk to them nor they to me. It was a terrible lesson to learn and one not soon forgotten.

I have used this story in a more abbreviated form to talk about the consequences of sin. My father did not see me disobey him but he knew that I had. Then I added lying to my sin. That sin led to being cut off from the family. I was still alive, but dead to the family.

I would then ask listeners if they had ever been exiled or put out of their family or community because of some wrong doing. Some had. They could relate to a story like this even though it happened in another culture. As a son I had shamed by father by lying to him. I had been justly punished. Then I was restored to the family.

In many of these cultures it is a terrible thing to be exiled or excluded by the community. So that aspect of the story resonated with them. In the Bible there are several stories that tell of separation. The story of Adam and Eve begins the exile stories. Then Cain is sent away from his people and the presence of the Lord. Another story is that of Miriam's rebellion against Moses and her becoming leprous as a result, and being excluded outside the camp.

In the story of David and Absalom, after Absalom killed his brother Amnon, he exiled himself to the King of Geshur and remained there until David was persuaded to bring him back to Jerusalem. Even then David refused to see Absalom in a kind of excommunication which led to a later rebellion by Absalom. Finally Jesus tells of the coming separation due to unbelief and sin. The story of Lazarus and the Rich Man is an example.

LifeStories Must Be Culturally Appropriate

I had to learn how to be sensitive to what kinds of stories were best to tell my listeners in their own cultures. Many of my stories would not make sense in their cultures. Even worse, some would be offensive or totally counter to the message.

In an unfortunate incident a guest speaker from the U.S., who is an excellent author and well-published, had come to Singapore to teach at the seminary. He was invited to be the featured speaker on a mass rally night for the local Baptist churches. As his main illustration the speaker used a hypothetical story about a man who happened to see some nice furniture being thrown away in a trash bin. The man went and salvaged it and brought it to his home and was very proud of it.

While I could appreciate this as an American who despises the waste of good, usable items, the problem was the inappropriateness of this story for Singaporeans who routinely discard as trash what others would consider still useable. And the very thought of going to the refuse bin to retrieve something that another had already used was not acceptable in their culture. Unfortunately, this story was the pivotal part of this speaker's message. Some of the Singaporeans around me were clearly uncomfortable and embarrassed at this gaffe by an inappropriate story.

I, too, must confess to having used inappropriate stories early in my missionary service before I learned the need for understanding the worldviews of my listeners. The point was reinforced even more strongly after involvement with Bible Storying. Several times, even in the midst of telling a Bible story I realized that it was not going over very well with my listeners. I realized that their failing to follow the story was because of cultural or social differences that were not the norm for my listeners.

The best thing to happen with inappropriate stories is that the listeners are not able to understand at all because they have no context or frame of reference. Continuing down the scale would be those stories that are not understood as intended but instead of proving a good illustration rather led to further confusion or doubt.

Next would be stories that innocently led to an increase in hostility or feeling by the listeners that you are an unworthy person or hostile person or that Christianity is not good. And the absolute last thing you want to happen is for stories to be considered grossly inappropriate or embarrassing like the story of the furniture rescued from the refuse bin. I might add that in some cultures stories can embarrass listeners who feel shame for the one telling the inappropriate story.

Over a period of 35 years working with peoples in some 24 countries who are non-Western, non-Christian, and sometimes non-friendly to Americans, I have learned what stories I can and cannot tell in most places. In addition to the content or storyline, I have learned that some stories, no matter how good or appropriate, just do not translate well into another culture without lengthy explanations to qualify the story. Humorous stories are sometimes the most difficult to translate and preserve the humor. In most cases, Bible Storyers are well advised to use humorous stories only with great care.

Swapping Stories with Listeners

By considering many of these implications, over time I was able to refine my "tellable" stories to a list that I had proved out and found to be appropriate, understandable, and usually translatable. The basic storyline, the details that I shared or withheld, the vocabulary I used, and even the manner in which I told the story all affected its reception.

The good outcome is that many of the peoples I worked with enjoyed hearing one of my stories as it gave them a means to remember me. I often swapped stories with them during our relaxed times as a way of letting them know me and for me to know them better.

So beyond the Bible stories I frequently used, I needed to search through my own personal stories to find relational stories that my listeners could relate to and not reject the story or receive a wrong idea from it. Since my mother grew up on a farm and I often visited the farm in my early years there were many anecdotes and illustrations I could use with the mostly rural people I was sharing the Bible stories with.

Opportunities to do this came when I realized that by swapping stories with my listeners I could develop a relationship with them by allowing them to own one of my stories and for me to own one of their stories. This worked well in the beginning. But as I worked with an ever growing circle of peoples, I had to remember more and more stories.

When I would first arrive and it was tea time they would recall my story. "Do you remember our story?" they asked. I had to start making notes and reviewing my who-told-what story notes before arriving. Later as I corresponded with those who interpreted for me or accompanied me on the teaching sessions I would try to recall some incident that happened, or story they told, and review it in the letter. This was a way of saying, "I haven't forgotten you after leaving." This leads into the next characteristic of stories: stories are memorable.

Stories are Memorable

After moving to Fort Worth I had found work with the Southern Baptist Radio and Television Commission. Several years earlier, while still in Louisiana, the director of that agency preached at my home church. His sermon that morning was the most graphic account of the Flood Story that I had ever heard. I was mesmerized by the details and imagery.

That story literally came alive and was for that hour happening right then and there as he told it. From that day over 51 years ago I remember the story and how powerful it was. I can't retell it as powerfully and with the same imagery that Paul Stevens did, but memory of that event and story lives on.

Another memorable story that Paul Stevens told his staff was so graphic that it is hard not to remember. I wish he were here to retell it for the reader in his own words. He told it as one of his own LifeStories. Here is his story as I remember it:

"I was serving as a chaplain with the Army Air Force in Italy. One day I received a call from the local aerodrome to come quickly to the field as one of the returning B-17 bombers was in trouble and was soon to attempt a landing. Upon arrival I found that the situation was far more serious as the situation was explained to me. The bomber had its hydraulic system shot out and so could not lower its landing gear. Why hadn't the crew bailed out I thought? Then the explanation continued.

The young belly gunner was in the lower gun turret under the plane when the damage occurred, and now because of the hydraulic system problem the turret could not be retracted into the bomber so he could get out. Now I began to understand the problem. This young man was trapped and facing a certain death in only a few minutes.

The controller was handing the microphone to me now and asking if I would talk to the young man over the radio. The bomber was out of fuel and was coming down. 'Chaplain, speak to the young man and comfort him.'

The bomber was now in sight and approaching the field getting lower and lower. I began, "Our Father who art in heaven." The bomber continued to drop toward the runway. "Hallowed be thy name. Thy kingdom come, thy will be done just as it is in heaven." The crippled bomber was now only feet above the concrete. "Give us this day our daily bread." The metal of the turret was beginning to scrape on the unyielding concrete of the runway. "Forgive us our trespasses, just as we forgive those who trespass against us."

Now the bomber was settling on its belly, sparks were flying and the turret was being torn apart and ground to pieces in the press between plane and ground. "Lead us not into temptation but deliver us from evil." The fire trucks were rolling toward the slowing plane where it was finally skidding to a stop. "For thine is the kingdom and the power forever. Amen." The boy was now gone, in God's hands. I handed the microphone back to the controller and slipped out of the tower. It had all happened in the matter of a few moments. I never forgot that terrible moment."

We didn't forget that moment either. Tears had welled up in Paul Stevens' eyes as he recalled his story. Stories are relational sometimes not because we are like the people in the story, or what happened to the people in the story, but because of our empathy with the characters, or with the storyteller.

I did not know the young man in the story. I've never been in a bomber. But I sensed the emotion and tension of that moment as Stevens told the story. We may in jest say that a story "yanked our chain." But, seriously, stories can do that.

Many times I have told the Passion Story of Jesus in what we call a fast-track method. I begin the story at some entry point before the Last Supper and continue through all the scenes and dialogue of the events up to the Ascension without stopping for comment or discussion. It is a relatively long story and can take up to an hour or more to tell.

How do I remember that long story? In the beginning it was hard to do. I needed to have my Bible handy for reference. But as I have told the story over and over as a presentation or a class demonstration I have learned to stand "in the story" figuratively and simply recount for the listeners what I am seeing and hearing happening all around me.

For those moments the story is alive and happening right then. I am sensing it and sharing it as I sense it. It is difficult to tell the crucifixion details without feeling the fear and pain, smelling the blood and sweat of the condemned, and being deeply moved emotionally every time. That story has become very relational for me as I have in my telling been part of the story. If you are really caught up in reliving a story as you tell it, you also can have this experience. Finding yourself in the midst of the story is one of the more rewarding experiences in Bible storying.

Not All Our Stories Are Sad

I did have a humorous story experience while in India. I was staying at a guest house with an older missionary couple. The husband was a counselor who was training some of the hospital staff. He loved to tell stories but he told them slowly at great length in excruciatingly minute detail.

One morning as we had breakfast together he began one of his stories which was looking like it might never end. Finally his longsuffering wife chimed in, "For heavens sake, J..., finish your story. This man needs to go to work!"

Stories are High Touch

Today we live in a high tech world surrounded by devices that allow us to exist in our own little environment of sound and entertainment and to reach out to others even though distanced by the technological gadgets we so frequently use. But though we enjoy so many benefits of *high tech*, inwardly we long for *high touch*. Now I realize that a phone call home to one's parents is a way of touching them. But a live visit is a much greater touch. In a micro way, we also express and experience high touch when we listen to their stories as well as share our stories.

Hurting people need touch. Stories are emotional as well as informative. They can resonate in the hurting heart. The old saying, "Misery loves company" should be eclipsed by a better saying, "Caring enough to listen brings joy to the hurting heart."

Some years ago Dr. John Drakeford, who taught Counseling at Southwestern Baptist Theological Seminary in Fort Worth, published a book titled, *The Awesome Power of the Listening Ear*.[24] He was right. The listening ear is very powerful as it signals acceptance, a willingness to take the time to hear your story—joining your life in doing so, to be a friend, to be a good listener.

Help! Is Anybody Listening?

While living in the Philippines, I would from time to time go out to visit fellow missionaries. I had a dual purpose. One, it gave me a chance to get out of the studio and office and experience the culture, especially in rural areas. Two, it gave me a chance to spend time with missionaries who lived in remote places, working in isolation away from their fellow missionaries.

As a new missionary on the field I observed that many of these rural and scattered missionaries would come to the annual mission meetings hurting from loneliness or just wanting to share with someone what was happening where they lived and worked. Their stories, needs and hurts many times were outside the interest and understanding of those who worked in urban areas or the various institutions.

In my role as a media developer, I had no administrative role over these fellow missionaries. When I visited their areas and stayed in their homes they wanted to talk — actually do *show and tell*. I learned to do *watch and listen*. What I saw and heard was for me and not for reporting to anyone else. So a level of trust evolved. I learned to ask questions like "How is the family doing?" or "What projects are you working on now?" and let them talk.

Some of their stories I could appreciate; others I did not always understand. Some I did not agree with. But I listened. In time my work area increased to include other Asian countries and a wider diversity of missionaries and nationals. I heard stories about personal needs and family situations because in my role I did not represent authority, or it was perceived that I would not judge a person because of their personal stories.

I remember one incident involving a newly appointed couple who had finally made it to the mission field after some struggle in school. I can easily identify with the man because I was not very good in learning a new language either. The couple was posted to an isolated place and committed to full time language study. It wasn't going well for the husband.

One day I happened to be present when his language supervisor, I suppose innocently asked how his language study was progressing. The man exploded, "All you ever do is ask about my language study! No one ever asks about me! Doesn't anyone care about me?"

The couple did not finish their term. It was obvious they felt a sense of isolation and believed the mission's only interest was in how well they were progressing in language study. Someone needed to listen to their LifeStory.

Stories Are Distilled Spirit

Anne Morrow Lindberg in her book *Bring Me a Unicorn*,[25] defined one's letters as "distilled spirit." Stories, too, are distilled life spirit as the events of one's life are selectively collected into a narrative and shared. We distill the plethora of life events, thoughts, and verbal exchanges into LifeStories. These distilled stories provide windows through which people can understand us, accept our stories, and follow us to the stories of Jesus.

Distorted Stories

Sometimes people do strange things with their LifeStories. Have you ever met someone who consistently told another person's stories as their own? I know someone who has written himself into some of my stories and shared them as his stories. In some of the stories he was obviously too young at the time to be that person.

This practice was caught by another person who knew me and my stories and reported the fact to me. I suppose that I am honored by having such interesting stories that someone would want to try them on as their own. But I am saddened to think that person has chosen to lay aside his own stories and see in my stories a better story to be in.

Devoid of Stories

There are people who feel they have no story to tell. In her book *Performance of Emotion Among Paxtun Women*, Benedicte Grima tells of the practice of Pashtun women to gather for the express purpose of sharing their personal misfortune stories as a means of garnering emotion from their women listeners.

One young schoolteacher was asked by Grima in her research about her own LifeStory. She replied, "I have no story to tell. I've been through no hardships." [26] The storytelling sessions were often dominated by the older women who had "more hardships and suffering and so more stories to tell."

I've actually experienced this when talking with someone who had nothing to say. It takes patience to wait them out. I've tried telling some of my stories that I thought would kindle a response or inspire the person to share one of their stories, but to no luck. I've tried asking questions to see if I could provoke a story.

Loss of Stories

I observed this loss of story among my children who grew up over a fifteen year period while living in the Philippines. There they had very full lives. During those years I heard them exchanging stories about their school, some of the antics on the school buses, mapping out all the fruit trees in our neighborhood, and stories from their classmates whose parents worked in exotic places.

When they returned to the U.S., however, two of them lost their stories, perhaps because they were overwhelmed by new experiences and the new stories simply displaced the Philippines stories. But over time they have recovered some of their stories and enjoy getting together and swapping these recovered stories. But for most of us, stories are memorable as containers of events, talk and scenes that were part of our lives at some time past.

Memorable Stories

When I began writing this part of the book my mother was still living at 94. She was still agile and mentally alert. During our visits with her she would often begin telling one of her stories about the people who lived in the small rural community where she grew up. She often repeated her stories as she had for a number of years, reliving her life through her stories.

On a whim one time I printed out the cemetery listing from several of the rural cemeteries where she had lived. This may sound like a bizarre thing to do for an elderly person in the twilight years of her life. But not to worry, my mother studied those lists of names which then triggered a flood of stories about those long dead relatives and neighbors of that rural community. She admitted that she had not thought about some of them for a long time, but seeing their names reminded her of the times they came visiting, shared meat after killing a beef, or their family crises.

Though I have heard most of the stories too many times to count, I was often surprised when my mother slipped in a new story that I had not heard before. That rural community no longer exists except in the stories about it. With few exceptions her stories revolved around relatives and the young people who lived on neighboring farms.

One sad story she has recounted several times is that of a cousin who lived on a nearby farm and apparently was his contemporaries' life of the party. He was always entertaining the others, standing on a stump giving a speech, or some other antic performed to the delight of all. One day when he was sixteen he came down with appendicitis and by the third day was dead. I share his name as my middle name. Other stories were happier as my mother recalled the times when relatives came to pick blackberries that grew wild along the field fences.

Mother often recalled all the relatives and the degree of relation and mentioned where they were buried. I don't know of anyone I know today who understands all these intricate relationships like she did. And she remembered stories about all of them! Another cemetery list I found later was from an older cemetery and to her delight she found the name of a relative that she had been trying to recall for a long time and you guessed it, another story!

Your LifeStory

Dr. Sánchez has written about the things to consider in your LifeStory in order to be prepared when God gives you the opportunity to minister to another through the experiences that God has given you. Your own LifeStories are unique. At the same time, however, you may find that your stories interestingly parallel the stories of others. Every Christian should realize that he/she has a LifeStory that God can use in the sharing of His message.

What is even more interesting is that there are patterns that seem to repeat. In the field of writing there are some thirty-six basic plots that occur over and over with many varying details. These basic plots make up the framework of writing stories for books and performing media.

Repeating Patterns in Life Stories

Swapping stories is a way we have of relating to others, seeing that while our exact lives may be different, they are alike in many ways. There are patterns that are repeated over and over again in our lives. For me as a missionary leaving the U.S. to go and live in a foreign country, I only thought about the task I was to do and our family survival in their new culture. It was sometime before I began to realize that other missionaries shared some of the same interests and life events that I did.

Because my assigned work involved travel to other countries for projects and training, I became acquainted with missionaries outside of the country and mission where I lived. Many things happened in those other countries that became part of my story. Some of these were quite humorous and may one day wind up in a book on the lighter side of missions. But what I enjoyed most was finding that the patterns in my life were repeated in the lives of others. Following is a piece that I wrote some time back that reflects on these repeating LifeStory patterns that we find in our shared stories.

The LIFE Quilt

When I was a boy families had quilts on their beds in the wintertime. These were not "store-bought" quilts, these were "hand-made" quilts. Almost every family had several. Most people today would think of comforters or blankets, but in those days we had quilts. They graced our beds in the cold days of winter and were carefully folded and stored during the warm summer months.

Do you know how quilts are made? Have you ever seen a quilting frame? Do you know about the several popular patterns that make up the pieces that are stitched together to form the quilt?

I was a child during the 1940s, growing up in a small Louisiana town. My mother's parents lived on a farm some twenty miles away. During the summers of those early years I would ride with the rural mail carrier on his route and get out at my grandparents' farm.

The house was a large cypress plank house with high ceilings. I can even remember when it had no wallpaper and bare wooden floors. The walls were bare wood and had splinters, too, as I painfully remember.

In the large room with a fireplace that we would call a living room hung a framework suspended from the ceiling. I asked about that thing and was told it was a quilting frame. I wondered what on earth it was used for and even how it was used so high up in the air. It never occurred to me that it would be lowered so the ladies could sit around it and sew those threads that tied the back cover to the stitched together front.

My grandmother kept a sewing basket with pieces of strangely cut cloth and usually there was a growing stack of square and sometimes other shapes of cloth sewed together in some kind of a pattern. I asked her one day what she was sewing. "I'm making a quilt," she replied. "I sew all these little pieces together into a pattern and then I sew all the big pieces together." Well, that was interesting but did not fully answer my curiosity until one day I saw where all this sewing was heading.

All of the small pieces had been sewed into the big pieces and the big pieces were now assembled on her foot pedal Singer sewing machine. On the appointed day some friends of my grandmother arrived and after they had coffee and small talk about their families I saw the "thing," the quilting frame, being lowered down. It hung on four ropes attached at the corners. First a large piece of cloth was carefully stretched out on the frame. Then cotton batting (I thought that was a strange word!) was laid on top of the backing cloth. Finally I began to see where this was heading when my grandmother proudly unfolded the big piece she had been piecing together and with great care and help from her friends positioned it on the top of the layered batting.

Then the ladies went to work hand sewing the edges of the two pieces of cloth together and tying the top and bottom covers at intervals with some colorful embroidery thread and little brightly colored pieces of cloth where the threads came up and were tied. It took a couple of hours for the ladies to finish the task. I learned later this was called a "quilting bee." At last the new quilt was removed from the frame and held up for all to inspect. Then it was carefully folded and put away for use when winter arrived.

If you are still reading perhaps you are wondering where this story is going? What fascinated me beyond the frame and all the activity of sewing the quilt were the patterns of the squares that made up the quilt. In this particular one the repeating pattern was the likeness of a doll wearing a bonnet. I recall other quilts that had star patterns, sun flowers, or something like a fat plus sign, or small squares that looked like a spinning geometric pattern. Several interesting observations arose from studying these quilts.

First, the patterns, though not necessarily composed of identical color and pattern cloth were repeated over and over in the quilt. It was like a cycle of events, or images that emerged again and again. Second, I realized that when I studied other quilts these same basic designs often were there, though the colors and patterns of the small pieces of cloth were different. But when joined together they made up a quilt just like the other quilts I studied.

There was yet another interesting thing to learn. It happened when I overheard my grandmother and some of the ladies discussing the quilt. "These pieces of gingham are from Ruth's dress when she was little. Now the red flowerdy (*sic*) pattern is from a feed sack," she was telling the ladies.

Every piece of cloth seemed to have its own story or represented something that she remembered. Wow! I thought that quilt is a memorial to all those things. She has joined it into a picture. It was at this point that I learned something about life.

You see, our lives are like that quilt. There are patterns that repeat themselves over and over as we live out our days. Many of these patterns come from our own families and are established in our early years of childhood. Other patterns come as we grow into adulthood and are related to living in a new family with our spouses, with our friends and even with the work we do and the people we work with. Because we are who we are, the little designs, though obscure at times, repeat themselves.

At last our quilt is finished when life is done. For many the quilt is there to be viewed by relatives and acquaintances. And if you happen to be famous, or decide to write a book about yourself, your "life quilt" is on display for all to see.

Reviewing a Story

Recently I attended the memorial service for the wife of a fellow missionary. As part of the service her life was reviewed in story (anecdotes, accomplishments), and via pictures. It was a review of her story from early home life to the pinnacle of her career as a denominational leader followed by declining health, though still active in her personal ministries until her life was finally taken by a massive stroke. A whole LifeStory told and reviewed in less than two hours. How many stories were simply compressed into that time frame!

When my wife and I were seeking appointment as missionaries and writing out our life stories we were discovering those patterns. There were similar patterns in our own lives as we each were the older sibling. Later while living among other missionaries from our own organization and from those with other organizations we realized there were repeating patterns in their stories like those in our stories.

Even more amazing, as I visited in Asian homes and got to know Asian families and co-workers, I found that many of them had stories similar to mine. The fine details were different because of our different cultures. But a recognizable similarity between western and Asian stories was clear.

As I have learned to listen to people share their stories and in turn to share selected portions of mine, I have learned to look for those patterns. Often the recognition is expressed in the words, "You know, something like that also happened to me." At that point we connect, our stories intersect. There is a bonding of stories for that moment and often continuing as we keep in touch.

But it is when I'm with other missionaries whose stories so closely parallel mine that the stories really begin to flow! This is really true among those who have worked in the same countries or situations I worked in.

Looking back at the years of travel I do rejoice at the good sharing times and how much richer my life is because of listening to my colleagues. And I rejoice at their interest in my stories as well. The stories of each became merged into "our stories."

During my days of working among Asian peoples I began to collect their hats. Today in retirement I have an assortment of their hats on my study wall and in several other rooms. Those hats all have a story about the people who gave them to me when they heard that I collected hats. Beyond the hats are the many people in those cultures whose stories briefly intersected with mine for a season.

When women missionaries in Indonesia reached retirement the other women in the mission used to stitch together a memory quilt that included scenes and sayings of their days in that country. Also Scriptures would be stitched into the quilt. The quilt would be presented to the retiree in ceremony. Those quilts were not as intricate as my grandmother's quilts, but were just as memorable. Such a quilt hangs on the wall in the missionary house of my church here in Texas.

Unfortunately in today's fast pace of life and bombardment with so much entertainment, it is easy to lose sight of our own LifeStory and our "little stories," most of which are never known by others.

We grow older and, because of many triggering events, some of those previously untold stories and even secret stories come out. Many of these have to do with hurts or embarrassments we suffered in our early years.

Our marriage and work stories displace many of those early stories which, unless something calls attention to them, tend to dim into our distant past. Our work stories and the stories of our families and those we correspond with become the story of the day.

Back to the quilt. Your LifeStory is also a quilt of little stories, often joined in repeating patterns, all joined into your own LifeStory. How many of these stories parallel the stories of others? How many of these stories would help you to empathize with another whose stories are not so happy? Do you need to unfold your LifeStory quilt and take a look at it? Could at least a part of it be spread out before someone so they could see the patterns of your life—especially the patterns of how God has blessed you in the good times and covered you with His grace during the difficult times? Where your LifeStories intersect is a good place to allow God's Story of forgiveness of sin and salvation through faith in Jesus to be a part of you and your listener's LifeStory Encounter.

When thinking about sharing in LifeStory encounters we look for the relational stories as we connect and we look to the good stories to show there is hope with a measure of God's grace to get through life.

Your Greatest LifeStory

We may have many touching and powerful LifeStories which we can share. But our greatest LifeStory is our personal encounter with Jesus Christ as our Savior. This is a very personal story of that moment when we realized our sinful condition and our need for forgiveness and faith in Jesus Christ as our Savior.

Not all these salvation stories will be the same. Some fear that their salvation LifeStory is not as powerful or dramatic as that of another who had a real "Damascus Road" type of encounter. While these stories are very powerful and dramatic, they can also put off that person who would respond more to the "Quiet Garden" type of salvation encounter.

I have enjoyed the rich experience of asking the people in the countries where I lived and worked to tell me about the time when they met Jesus Christ as their Savior. For some it was a short story of how they heard the Gospel and felt the Holy Spirit's call to salvation. For others because of their family's religious background there was often a struggle due to fear of persecution or rejection by their families.

One young Indian man who was pastor of a church my wife and I attended while living in Singapore told of his call to salvation and what happened as a result. When he told his family of his desire to follow Jesus and be baptized, a Hindu priest put a curse on him telling him that the day he was baptized his grandmother would die. He struggled with his decision not only to put his faith in Christ but to follow in obedience in baptism. He prayed for wisdom and for God to break the curse.

At last he felt that he had peace about the matter and was baptized. That same day he received word that his grandmother was taken seriously ill, in danger of dying and was in the hospital. He hurried back to be with her and have a prayer vigil that the curse be broken. In time the grandmother improved and lived. He had other LifeStories that reflected his Indian culture and faith in Jesus.

Others who shared their salvation LifeStories with me told how they found a tract while riding on a bus and, as they read it, realized they were sinners in need of a Savior. While riding on the bus they prayed silently to receive forgiveness and salvation through faith in Jesus. Their stories were simple and not dramatic, but perhaps in a way more typical and easy to relate to.

One of the most dramatic salvation LifeStories I heard came from a young man during a Bible storying training conference in Bali. Because I frequently heard stories from people about how Jesus had appeared to them in a dream, I would usually at some point while conducting Bible storying training would ask the group if any had dreams in which Jesus appeared to them. In this group of thirty there were six who told of such dreams. But the one I have continued to remember went something like this:

"During my life I realized that I possessed certain abilities and powers. So I became a *dukun* (witchdoctor) and over a period of time came into bondage to over 150 evil spirits that gave me wisdom and power. But one night I had a strange dream in which a person dressed in white appeared in my dream and told me, "You are dirty. You must bathe in clean water."

The person did not identify himself. Over a period of time there were other visitations by a person dressed in white. I was troubled by these dreams and the spirits that I was in bondage to did not like the dreams. At last in another dream a person appeared who identified himself as Jesus and said that I must leave the evil spirits and follow him only.

I wanted to do this but a terrible struggle ensued over a long period of time as the spirits did not want to release me. At last the final bond was broken and I was free to follow Jesus. I knew he wanted me to tell others about him. So now I am in Bible school preparing myself for this work."

Others in the group told of their fears about leaving the family and village deities to follow Jesus. Some told of how they brought a chicken sacrifice to the local village gods to beg the deities not to harm them as they left following the deity to instead follow Jesus. Also they asked that the gods not harm their family or disturb the village harmony.

These LifeStories were helpful to me to understand the struggles they faced in coming to Jesus Christ as savior. I was able to benefit from this information in my teaching about the use of Bible Storying in ministry. I appreciated their willingness to share these stories with me—an outsider to their culture and one who would only be with them a brief time for the training. The Bible Storyer will find that people will be willing to share their stories and that these times of sharing can open doors for sharing Bible stories.

Summary

Each person should be aware of a whole library of personal stories that exist. The most important one is the story of one's personal encounter with Christ as Savior. With a little reflection other stories can be recovered from one's memory. A helpful exercise could be to outline one's life. Then go back and revisit each scene or happening to envision what happened, what was on the heart at that moment, what was learned from the event? Then reflect on how each event came to be. Where were you when it happened? Who was involved or near when the story occurred? What did the event mean to you afterward? To others who were involved in the story?

In the same way reflect on times with others and the events that happened. Make it a point to be sensitive to hear the stories that others share. If necessary, share your story (ies) and listen to theirs. Soon your library of stories will grow giving you a rich heritage from which to draw and share when you have that precious time of listening and share LifeStories in a God-given ministry moment.

One last thought. It is wise to be prudent in how your own LifeStory relates to the one you'd just heard. The object is not to top their story, besting it with grander or more poignant events, but to somehow relate to it, and through your story bridge to the story from God's Word. Your story then serves a valuable function of providing that connection, that transition from their story expressing their heart to God's Story, expressing His heart.

CHAPTER 5

BRIDGING BIBLE STORIES

J.O. Terry & Daniel Sánchez

Throughout the book we have given some suggestions about Bible stories that can be used as bridges to enable people to understand the story of Jesus more clearly. In order to assist storyers, we are including these stories in this chapter. We want to encourage storyers to feel free to adapt the vocabulary to the persons who hear the stories.

We also want to underscore that this is by no means a complete list of all the Bible stories that can be used as bridges in storying encounters. Some of these stories have been compiled from different portions of Scripture in light of the fact that they are not found in one single chapter or portion of the Bible. Nonetheless, the content of these stories is strictly biblical and represents a composite picture of the character in the story.

Please note that these stories are not in chronological order. They simply appear in the order in which they were listed in the earlier chapters of this book. Also note that these stories have been presented in the simplest and briefest way possible. The reason for this is to focus on the main lesson of the story and to share it in such a way that it will be a bridge for people to understand the Story of Jesus with clarity, power, and interest. The book, *Basic Bible Stories,* presents principles for simplifying the stories so people can more easily understand them.[27]

It is also important to point out that some of these stories (e.g., Esther, Prodigal Son) can be used in connection with more than one of the themes that we have included in this chapter. We want you to feel free to adapt the manner in which you connect each of these stories to the story of Jesus. We also want you to either reduce or expand the content of the stories to fit the setting in which you are telling them.

Remember, the main purpose for these stories is that they serve as a bridge to the Story of Jesus. You will want to seek the guidance of the Holy Spirit as you decide which stories to use and how to share them. You will also want to keep clearly in mind the ultimate objective of presenting the story of Jesus. The stories will appear under the following themes:

Joys and Achievements

- David and Goliath (1 Sam 17)
- Esther (Est 2-7)
- Joyful News from the Angels (Luke 2)
- Jesus at the Wedding Celebration (John 2)
- **Life-Shaping Influences**
- Naomi and Ruth (Ruth 1-4)
- David and Jonathan (1 Samuel)
- Barnabas and John Mark (Acts, Epistles)
- Paul and Timothy (Acts, Epistles)
- **Sorrows and Difficulties**
- Jesus Calms the Storm (Matt 8)
- Jesus Heals the Blind Man (John 9)
- Jesus Heals the Demon Possessed Boy (Matt 17)
- Jesus Raises Lazarus (John 11)
- Changes and challenges:
- Joseph (Book of Genesis)
- David and Goliath (1 Samuel 17)
- Esther (Book of Esther)

- Daniel (Book of Daniel)
- Mary, Joseph, and Jesus Escape to Egypt (Matt 2)
- The Prodigal Son (Luke 15)

Joys and Achievements
David and Goliath
(I Samuel 17)

The story of David and Goliath is a dramatic account of the victories people can achieve when they trust in God.

David was the youngest of the sons of Jesse. His brothers were old enough to serve in King Saul's army, but, David, because of his youth, had to stay home and take care of his father's sheep. One day Jesse sent David to the camp where King Saul's army was staying. David was to take food to his brothers and find out how they were doing.

When David arrived he noticed that Saul's army was lined up across the valley from the army of the enemy, the Philistines. While David was talking with his brothers, Goliath, a giant, came out from the line of the Philistines and started shouting and challenging King Saul to send a soldier to fight against him. When Saul's soldiers saw this they became afraid and ran off.

David then asked: "Who does that worthless Philistine think he is to insult the armies of God? I will go out and fight him myself." When the soldiers heard this, they went and told Saul. When Saul saw David he said, "You are only a boy, and he is a soldier with great experience."

David then told the King that when he was on the fields as a shepherd with God's help he was able to defend his sheep from lions and bears and other wild beasts. He added: "I know that the Lord will protect me from the hands of this Philistine." The King then told him, "Go and fight and I hope that the Lord will protect you."

David then went to a stream and picked out five smooth stones and put them in his leather bag. Then with his sling in his hand he went out to meet Goliath. When the giant saw him, he started making fun of him saying: "Do you think I'm a dog that you should come after me with sticks. I am going to kill you and feed your body to the wild animals."

David then said: "You come to fight with me with a spear, a dagger, and a sword. I will fight you in the name of God the one who has all the power."

When Goliath started going forward, David put a stone in his sling and started swinging it. When he let go of one of the straps the stone flew out and hit Goliath in the forehead. Goliath then fell facedown and David went and with the giant's own sword cut his head off. When the King's soldiers saw this, they started chasing after the Philistine army and defeated these enemies.

After that great victory, there was a great celebration with singing and dancing because of David's victory over the giant.

Note: Make a connection with the fact that with the power of our Lord Jesus Christ we can attain many victories in our lives.

Joyful News from the Angels
(Luke 2)

In the Bible we find many instances in which people experienced genuine joy. One of these occasions was when the angels gave the shepherds the great news that Jesus, the Messiah, had been born. This is the way the story is told in the Bible.

When Mary and Joseph were in Bethlehem, the time came for Jesus to be born. Mary then gave birth to her first born son and wrapped him in a blanket and laid him on a manger because there was no room for them in the inn.

That night shepherds were watching over their flocks of sheep. Suddenly an angel appeared before them and the brightness of the glory of God surrounded them. The shepherds became frightened. The angel then said to them: "Don't be afraid because I am going to give you some good news that will be for all people. Today, in King David's hometown a baby who is the Savior of the world has been born. This is how you will be able to know who he is. You are going to find the baby wrapped in a blanket and lying on a manger."

Suddenly other angels appeared and said: "Glory to God in the highest and on earth peace to all men." After the angels disappeared, the shepherds said: "Let's go to Bethlehem and find out what the Lord has told us about."

They ran as fast as they could and when they got there they found Mary and Joseph and the baby lying in the manger. The angels then returned to their fields joyfully thanking God because he is wonderful.

Note: Connect this story with experiences of joy. Use this as a bridge to present the story of Jesus. Notice how the joy of the Angels transferred to the shepherds as they responded to the promises of the Savior.

Jesus at the Wedding Celebration
(John 2:1-12)

The first recorded miracle Jesus performed was at a celebration. He and his disciples were invited to a wedding in the city of Cana of Galilee. It is quite likely that the family of the bride and the groom were either relatives or close friends of Jesus' mother Mary because she was at the feast.

At that time wedding festivals lasted several days. In order that many people could wish them well, the bride and the groom were taken by their neighborhoods on the way to the place where the ceremony would take place. After the wedding ceremony the couple would remain to celebrate with the people. Because of the scarce resources among humble families, the wedding ceremony was a once-in-a-life time opportunity to celebrate to their hearts' content.

Since the celebration was so important to the couple as well as to their families, it was the custom to place a master of ceremonies in charge to make sure that everything went well. In this wedding things did not go well because they ran out of wine. When Jesus learned about this, he instructed the servants to fill the empty containers with water. Jesus then performed a miracle turning the water into wine. The wine was so good that the master of ceremonies asked why they had saved the best wine for the last.

The fact that Jesus attended this wedding and performed his first miracle there is indicative that He considers these types of celebrations important. It is also clear that the presence of Jesus in our celebrations adds an immeasurable amount of joy and meaning. This is consistent with what Jesus said: "I have come that you might have life and that you might have it to the fullest" (John 14:6).

Note: Use this story as a bridge to share the story of Jesus.

Life-Shaping Influences
Naomi and Ruth
(Ruth 1-4)

Sometimes great life-shaping influences can follow times of great sorrow if one is faithful and patient. In the following story the tragedies of death led to a life-changing relationship which in time worked out to bless two women and led to marriage for the young woman Ruth.

Naomi and her husband and two sons had left their homeland during a famine in search of food. They settled in the neighboring country of Moab where in time the two sons each married a Moabite woman. After some time had passed Naomi's husband died as did the two sons of Naomi leaving three childless widows.

Naomi decided to return to her own country and encouraged the two Moabite girls to return to their own families. One did, but the other named Ruth begged Naomi not to send her away. Instead Ruth said, "Don't urge me to leave you. Where you go I will go and where you stay I will stay. Your people will be my people and your God my God. May the Lord deal severely with me if anything but death separate us." So Naomi and Ruth returned to Bethlehem. Naomi was bitter about her experience and felt that the Lord had afflicted her.

The barley harvest was just beginning so Ruth asked to go to the fields and pick up the left over grain. As it turned out she went to the field of a relative of Naomi's dead husband. When the field owner Boaz asked about Ruth, the workers gave a good report about how diligently Ruth was working. So Boaz gave the order to protect Ruth and provide her with food and water. Ruth told Naomi about her experience and whose field she worked in.

One day after Naomi learned about Ruth's experience in meeting Boaz, she instructed Ruth how to go back to the threshing floor and during the night to lie down at the feet of Boaz. When Boaz awoke and discovered Ruth, he was pleased that she had chosen him and not one of the younger men. Early the next day Boaz went to the town gate to inquire if a nearer relative was interested to inherit Naomi's husband's field along with the widow Ruth. When the relative declined, then Boaz became the kinsman redeemer and took Ruth to be his wife.

The Lord enabled Ruth to conceive and give birth to a son. Then Naomi took the child and rejoiced because the other women were saying, "Your daughter-in-law, who loves you and is better to you than seven sons, has given birth to a son." And so Ruth became an ancestor of the great King David who was himself an ancestor of Jesus.

Note: Some events that happen in life are bitter experiences. These experiences can crush you. Such experiences can, however, lead to new relationships and unseen opportunities in the future that redeem your life and help you become a blessing to others. Such experiences can provide an enduring legacy for coming generations. Do not despise experiences that may seem difficult as such events will not destroy you.

David and Jonathan
(I Samuel 17)

Many of us know the story of how David killed Goliath, the giant. You may be interested in knowing about the deep friendship that developed between King Saul's son, Jonathan, and David.

After David returned from killing the giant, Jonathan developed such a deep admiration for David that he promised him that he would be his friend forever. As a token of his friendship Jonathan took off his robe and gave it to David. He also gave him his sword, his bow and arrows, and his belt.

David was so successful in everything King Saul asked him to do that he was made a high officer in his army. Everyone was so pleased that in each town that the army marched through on its way back from the battle the women sang: "Saul killed his thousands but David killed his ten thousands." This made Saul so jealous and angry that one day when David was playing his harp for King Saul, the King threw a spear at David, twice trying to kill him but David dodged.

In another attempt to get David killed, Saul sent him to lead his army against the enemy the Philistines. However, David led his army to victory.

When the King's plot did not work, Saul told his son Jonathan to kill David. Jonathan was such a good friend, however, that he warned David. After David learned of additional attempts on his life, he fled to the woods to escape from Saul. Jonathan then went out and found David and told him: "Tell me what I need to do to help you escape and I will do it."

Jonathan then returned to the place after promising David that he would find out what his father was plotting. Before leaving, Jonathan gave David a clue of the message he was going to send him about his father's intentions. He said: "I'm going to pretend that I am hunting in this area tomorrow. I will shoot three arrows. If I tell my servant 'the arrows are on this side, pick them up' it means that it is safe for you to come out of the cave where you are hiding," Jonathan then explained what the other signal would be: "If I tell my servant 'the arrows are farther away' it means that you must leave."

The next evening Jonathan followed the plan and gave David the signal that he needed to flee. After Jonathan's servant left, David came out an embraced Jonathan. They both cried. Jonathan then told David: "Remember that we have both asked the Lord to watch after us and that our descendents will keep our promise forever."

Years after that, Jonathan was killed in battle, Saul also died in battle, and David became King. When he ascended to the throne he did not forget the promise he made to his dear friend Jonathan. David asked: "Is anybody from Saul's family still alive. I promised Jonathan that I would be good to them."

David was then told that a son of Jonathan's named

Mephibosheth was alive and was crippled. David then made arrangements for Mephibosheth to eat at the king's table as long as he lived. This way David kept his promise to his beloved friend Jonathan who had saved his life.

Note: Point out the importance of genuine friendships. This can lead to the story of Jesus our very best friend.

Barnabas and John Mark
(Acts 13, 15; 2 Timothy)

John Mark's story inspires those of us who feel that we have made mistakes and desperately need a second chance.

The Apostle Paul and his colleague in ministry, Barnabas, met John Mark in the city of Jerusalem. John Mark was so excited about the missionary journeys that Paul and Barnabas were going to make that he volunteered to go with them as a helper.

Paul and Barnabas agreed to take John Mark on their very first journey. John Mark was very excited about being a part of the missionary team while the team was on the island of Cyprus. By the time they got to the second island, however, John Mark left the missionary team and went back home.

After a very successful trip to many cities, Paul and Barnabas went back to Antioch to the church that sent them. They decided to go on a second journey to visit the people they had talked to about Jesus, and to visit the churches they had started. Barnabas wanted John Mark to join the team once again. Paul, however, was so much against this that he decided to select another partner to go with him on the second trip.

John Mark was so grateful for Barnabas' trust in him that he became much more trustworthy. Many years later Paul was convinced that John Mark had learned so much from his past mistakes that he asked John Mark to join him in the city of Rome where Paul was a prisoner. Paul clearly stated that John Mark would be very useful to him in ministry. The fact that John Mark benefited greatly from Barnabas' trust and encouragement was also evident in the fact that John Mark wrote the Gospel of Mark.

Note: The story of John Mark reminds us of the fact that Jesus is willing to give us a second chance even after we have made some terrible mistakes. Tell the story of Jesus that relates to this truth of forgiveness and a chance to start over.

Paul and Timothy
(Acts, Romans, 1 & 2 Timothy)

Many times our lives are shaped by someone who mentors us, giving wise counsel and direction for our lives. Even more than just wise counsel it is wonderful if our mentor also shares with us how to live a life pleasing to God and that blesses many others we serve. Such was the relationship between the older Apostle Paul and the young disciple Timothy.

Paul was a Jew who was wise and instructed in the Law of God. In his early days he had persecuted Christians and even witnessed the death of faithful a young Christian who professed his belief in Jesus. Then Paul met Jesus in a vision and his life was changed. Paul began to travel beyond the borders of his own country he encountered many Greeks who were God-fearers. And many of these Greeks also became followers of Jesus.

A young Greek named Timothy had a godly grandmother and mother. Later Paul reminded young Timothy of the sincere faith which first lived in his grandmother Lois and in his mother Eunice. And Paul added that he was persuaded that Timothy had that same faith.

Paul visited the city where Timothy lived. Timothy was being discipled and the other believers spoke well of him. Paul wanted to take Timothy along on his journey. Paul had to circumcise Timothy because other Jews in that area knew that Timothy's father was a Greek. Later in their journey when Paul faced opposition and had to leave, Timothy and Paul's companion Silas stayed behind to continue the work. Later Paul sent two of his helpers which included Timothy to return to a place Paul had visited earlier.

When Paul wrote a letter to the believers in Rome, he mentioned Timothy as his fellow worker. Paul wrote two letters to Timothy encouraging him in his ministry, warning Timothy against false teachers and instructing Timothy regarding overseers and deacons. Paul also gave personal instruction to Timothy reminding Timothy of the things he must teach. He was to devote himself to the reading and preaching of the Scripture. He was not to let anyone look down upon him because he was young. And Paul added, "Do your best to present yourself to God as one approved, a workman who does not need to be ashamed and who correctly handles the word of truth."

Finally Paul said, "Continue in what you have learned and have been convinced of, because you know from who you learned it. I give you this charge: Preach the Word, always be prepared, rebuke and encourage with great patience."

What a wonderful example of a mentor and disciple. A devoted mentor can carefully instruct and guide his disciple to live a full and meaningful life that not only is fulfilling to the disciple but also is a great blessing and example to others. Every Christian should seek ways to serve as a mentor to others.

Changes and Challenges

Joseph

(Genesis 37-50)

In the Bible we find a story about a young man who faced many serious difficulties yet toward the end of his life he was able to look back and see the hand of God guiding him every step of the way.

Joseph was the eleventh of Jacob's sons. Jacob loved Joseph more than his other sons because Joseph was born in Jacob's old age. To show that he was his favorite Jacob gave Joseph a coat of many colors. Because of this, Jacob's brothers hated him.

One day when Joseph's brothers were in the pasture taking care of the sheep, Jacob sent him to go and find out how his brothers were. When Jacob's brothers saw Joseph they plotted to kill him, to throw Joseph in a pit, and to tell their father that a wild animal had killed him. Reuben, the oldest of the brothers, persuaded them not to kill Joseph but to throw him in a dry well, because Reuben was planning to go back and rescue Joseph. So when Joseph arrived, the brothers pulled off his coat of many colors and threw Joseph into a dry well.

While Reuben was gone, Jacob's brothers sold Joseph to a band of merchants who took him to Egypt. After that, the brothers took Joseph's coat, dipped it in the blood of a goat they had killed and told Jacob that Joseph had been killed by a wild animal. Jacob refused to be comforted saying he would go to his grave grieving his son's death.

When they arrived in Egypt, the merchants sold Joseph to Potiphar, the king's official in charge of the guards. Joseph did such a good job that Potiphar put him in charge of all of his house and all his property. Because Joseph was so handsome, Potiphar's wife asked him to make love to her. When Joseph repeatedly refused, she accused him of trying to attack her. When Potiphar heard the accusation, he had Joseph put in prison.

While in prison, Joseph, with God's help, interpreted the dreams of two of the king's officials who were also prisoners.

Two years later the king had a dream that no one could interpret. One of the officials who had been restored to the king's service then told the king about Joseph's ability to interpret dreams.

Joseph interpreted the king's dream and told him that there were going to be seven years of plentiful harvests followed by seven years of famine. The king was so impressed that he put

Joseph in charge of the palace and gave him authority to make provision so there would be sufficient food stored for the years of famine.

This famine reached the place where Jacob and his sons lived. Jacob then sent his sons to go to Egypt to buy grain. When they arrived the brothers did not recognize Joseph. At the right time Joseph revealed himself to the brothers. Joseph then told them: "Don't be afraid. I have no right to change what God has decided. You tried to harm me, but God made it turn out for the best, so he could save all the people, as he is now doing." (Genesis 50:19-20).

Point out that God can make something good come out of the worst of circumstances. Then tell the story of Jesus suffering on the cross, his death, and his resurrection which has resulted in salvation being available for those who believe (John 3:16).

Esther
(Book of Esther)

Esther was a Jewish girl who lived in exile in Persia. She became an orphan when she was very young. Her older cousin, Mordecai, raised her as his own daughter. Esther grew up to be a very beautiful young lady. Mordecai told her never to tell anyone that she was a Jew and she obeyed him.

One day King Xerxes sent out an order for the young women to present themselves before him so he could choose one as his queen. When the time came for Esther to present herself before the King, he liked her more than any of the other young women. Immediately he fell in love with Esther and crowned her his queen and had a great celebration.

Mordecai was a guard at the palace gate. While there, he found out that two of the other guards were planning to kill the King. Mordecai told Esther who in turn told the King. This saved the King's life.

The highest official in the palace, next to the king was Haman. He despised Mordecai because Mordecai would not bow before him when he passed through the palace gate. Haman's anger grew so much that he plotted to kill all of the Jews in the entire kingdom. To carry out this plot, Haman tricked the king into signing a letter that would let the citizens of the kingdom kill the Jews and take away their property.

When Mordecai found out about this letter he dressed like a grieving person and was crying publicly. Esther found out about this and sent a servant to talk to Mordecai. He gave the servant a copy of the order and said to her: "Show this to Esther and explain to her what it means. Ask her to go before the king and beg him to have compassion on her people, the Jews."

When Esther heard this she sent word back to Mordecai: "The king has a law that the queen is not to present herself before him if she has not been invited. The queen could be put to death if the king does not hold out his scepter to her."

Mordecai sent word to Esther saying: "It could be that you were made a queen for a time like this." Esther sent a message to Mordecai telling him to ask the Jewish people to pray for her. She said: "I will go in to see the King even if I must die."

Esther then dressed herself up in her royal robes went into the inner court in front of the palace and presented herself before the King. The King was very happy to see her and extended his golden scepter to her and asked her "Why have you come here? Tell me what you need and I will give you even half of my palace." Esther then invited the King and Haman to a dinner. At the dinner Esther told the King about the plot and that Haman was the one who planned it.

The King became so angry that he gave an order for Haman to be hanged. The King then gave an order for the Jews to defend themselves and protect their property. This spared the lives of the Jewish people. In order to celebrate this victory Queen Esther sent out a letter establishing the "Festival of the Purim" that the Jewish people celebrate to this day.

Note: Point out that even when we face severe challenges in our lives we can count on God's help to do the right thing and to be of help to others. Connect this with the story of Jesus who himself went through many severe challenges and came out victorious.

Daniel
(Book of Daniel)

As a young man Daniel was taken prisoner by the Babylonian army when the city of Jerusalem was conquered. When he and other young men from the tribe of Judah arrived in Babylon, King Nebuchadnezzar gave orders to his highest official telling him to choose some young men from the Jewish families. He said: "They must be healthy, handsome, smart, wise, educated and fit to serve the royal palace. Teach them how to speak and write our language and give them the same food and wine that I am served. Train them for three years, and then they can become my court officials" (Daniel 1:4-5).

Daniel was among the four young men chosen. Daniel, however made up his mind to eat and drink only what God had approved for his people to eat. Daniel then got permission from the guard in charge to eat only vegetables and water at meal times for ten days. At the end of the ten days Daniel and his friends looked healthier than the other young men who were given the King's food.

Later when Daniel with the help of God interpreted a dream that the king had had, he was promoted to a high position in the king's court and God was honored by Daniel's life. The King said: Now I know that your God is above all other gods and kings and he gave you power to explain this mystery" (Daniel 2:47).

When Babylon was conquered by Darius he became the new king. He made Daniel one of three officials in charge of the governors. Daniel did his work so much better than the others governors that they were jealous of him. As much as the other governors tried they could not find anything wrong because Daniel was honest and faithful. The only thing the other governors found that they could use was that Daniel prayed to God three times a day. The other governors then plotted to get the king to give an order that for the next thirty days no one should pray to any god or person except the king. The penalty would be that such a person would be thrown into a pit of lions.

As was his custom, Daniel prayed three times a day in front of a window that faced Jerusalem and gave thanks to God.

The other governors then told the king that Daniel had refused to obey the king's orders. The king was very sorry, but was trapped by the orders he had given, so he gave orders for Daniel to be thrown in the pit of lions. He said to Daniel: "You have been faithful to your God, and I pray that he will rescue you" (Daniel 6:16).

So Daniel was thrown in the pit of lions. That night the king could not sleep. Early in the morning he got up and went to the pit of lions. The king called out: "Daniel, you were faithful and served your God. Was he able to save you from the lions?" Daniel answered: "My God knew that I was innocent, and he sent an angel to keep the lions from eating me" (Daniel 6:21, 22).

Note: Daniel had many changes and challenges in his life but he always trusted God and The Lord never disappointed him. Jesus was tried in even more severe ways than Daniel so that is why he can understand what we go through and can help us in troubled times. We can trust Jesus to not only feel our needs but actually work in ways to help us meet and overcome any difficulty.

Mary, Joseph and Jesus Escape to Egypt
(Matthew 2)

Before Mary was due to give birth to her son, she and Joseph were required to go to Bethlehem to register for a census. So they left the town of Nazareth in Galilee and made the long journey to Bethlehem in Judea where the time came for Mary to give birth to a son as the angel had said would happen.

Though there was no room for Mary and Joseph in a proper lodging place, they found shelter in a place where animals were kept and placed her new born child in a manger. When the angels told the news of the Messiah's birth to shepherds nearby keeping watch over their flocks, they came to see the child and worship.

Sometime later when Mary and Joseph had found lodging in a house, Wise Men arrived from a foreign country after following an unusual star in the sky. The Wise Men had inquired from King Herod in Jerusalem about the one born King of the Jews. King Herod sent the Wise Men on their way but asked them to return and tell where they found the new King.

The Wise Men followed the star until it came to the house where Mary, Joseph, and the child Jesus were staying. Upon seeing the child, the visitors presented rich gifts befitting one born a King. After they had worshiped the child, the Wise Men were warned in a dream not to return to King Herod, but to return to their own country by another route.

Upon learning this, King Herod gave orders to kill all the boy babies in Bethlehem two years of age and younger. An angel appeared to Joseph in a dream saying, "Get up, take the child and his mother and escape to Egypt. Stay there until I tell you to return."

Immediately Joseph rose and took the child Jesus with his mother during the night and departed for Egypt where the family stayed until King Herod died. Then the angel again appeared in a dream to Joseph and said, "Get up. Take the child and his mother and return to the land of Israel." So Joseph obeyed the angel and took the child with his mother and returned to the land of Israel. Again Joseph was warned in another dream of the danger in Judea, he instead returned to Nazareth in the land of Galilee.

This story reminds us that life may be filled with changes and challenges that could affect our very lives. When God was gracious to warn Joseph about the danger and what he was to do, Joseph faithfully obeyed God. Though the changes were troublesome for Joseph and his family, it all worked out to fulfill prophecy, for their safety, and for God's glory.

The Prodigal Son
(Luke 15)

One day when Jesus was sharing with people the good news about the Kingdom of God, some tax collectors and sinners gathered around to hear him. When the Pharisees and teachers of the Law of Moses saw this, they were very displeased and said: "This man is friendly with sinners and even eats with them." When Jesus noticed this he told them some stories. One of the stories was about a man and his sons. This was the story he told.

A man had two sons. The younger son said to his father, "Give me my share of the inheritance." So the father divided the inheritance among his two sons. The younger son then took his belongings and left for a far away country where he wasted all his money on parties with his friends. After the younger son had spent everything, there was scarcity of food in that land and he found himself without friends and hungry. He then got a job taking care of pigs and he would have been glad to eat the pig's food but no one gave him any of it.

Then the son came to his senses and thought, "My father's workers have plenty to eat and I am here starving." He then thought to himself, "I am going to go back to my father and tell him: 'Father I have sinned against God and against you, I don't deserve to be your son anymore, please treat me as one of your servants.'"

So the son got up and went back to his father's home. When he got near, his father saw the younger son and felt sorry for him.

The father ran and hugged his son and kissed him. And the son said: "Father, I have sinned against God and against you."

But the father said to the servants, "Go and get the best clothes and put them on my son. Put a ring on his finger and shoes on his feet. Go and kill the best calf and prepare a feast so we can celebrate, because my son was dead and has come back to life, he was lost and has been found." And they began a great celebration.

This story told by Jesus reminds us of the love of God and of his willingness to forgive those who repent of their sins and seek to draw near to him. Jesus made this forgiveness possible through his death on the cross for our sins. The wonderful story speaks of the only way that sinful humans can receive the saving knowledge of Jesus Christ. It is the ultimate account of God's Grace to us. Tell the story of Jesus.

Sorrows and Difficulties

Jesus Calms the Storm
(Mark. 6; Matthew 14)

Many times we feel as if we were in the middle of a storm. These stormy times are more often in our emotions and feelings than physical storms. Often the waves of suffering, fears, and doubts hit our lives with such strength that we may wonder if we are going to survive.

That's exactly the way the disciples of Jesus felt one day. They had just seen Jesus perform a miracle in which he had fed a multitude of more than 5,000 by multiplying the fish and the bread. After that Jesus told his disciples to cross the lake on a boat and meet him on the other side.

Later that evening when the disciples were in the middle of the lake a furious storm came. The disciples were struggling very hard to row in order to try to get the boat ashore. At that point Jesus started toward them by walking on the water. When the disciples saw Jesus at a distance they became very scared and started screaming.

Jesus then came near to them and said: "Don't be scared I am Jesus." When Jesus got in the boat with them the winds died down and the water was very calm. The disciples then said: "You are really the Son of God" (Matthew 14: 33).

Jesus Heals the Blind Man
(Luke 18:35-42

One day Jesus was walking near the city of Jericho. Beside the road there was a blind man named Bartimaeus who was begging. When he heard all the commotion he asked what was going on. The people from the crowd told him that it was Jesus of Nazareth who was passing by. When Bartimaeus heard this, he began calling: "Jesus, son of David, have pity on me." The people around Bartimaeus told him to be quiet but Bartimaeus did not mind them. Instead he kept on calling: "Jesus son of David, have pity on me."

When Jesus heard this he stopped and told the people to bring Bartimaeus to him. When the blind man was near, Jesus asked him: "What do you want me to do for you?" Bartimaeus answered: "Lord, I want to see." Jesus then answered him: "Because you have faith you are healed. You can now see." Right away Bartimaeus could see. He was so grateful that he kept following Jesus and thanking God for his healing.

Note: Point out the fact that Bartimaeus had a strong faith in Jesus and did not give up even when the people around him told him to be quiet. It is this kind of faith that we need to draw near to Jesus with our needs, cares, fears, and sorrows. Use this as a bridge to focus on the story of Jesus.

Jesus Heals the Demon Possessed Boy

(Mark 9:14-29)

Jesus had just spent time with three of his disciples when they returned to where the other disciples were surrounded by a crowd. A man then came and fell down on his knees and begged Jesus: "Lord, have pity on my son. A demon keeps my son from talking, He is very ill. Often he falls into the fire and into the water. When the demon comes over my son he throws him onto the ground, makes his mouth to foam, and then makes him look as if he were dead." The man then said: "I brought my son to your disciples but they could not force the demon to come out."

Just as they were talking the boy fell and started rolling on the ground and foaming at the mouth. Jesus asked the father: "How long has this been going on?" The man replied; "Ever since he was a child. The demon has often tried to kill him by throwing him into the fire or into the water. Please have pity on us."

Jesus then said to the demon: "I order you to come out of the boy and never bother him again." The demon then came out screaming and the boy looked as if he were dead. But Jesus took him by the hand and helped him to stand up.

Note: This story can help underscore the fact that Jesus has absolute power over evil spirits and the devil himself. This can help people who have struggles with evil forces in their lives and feel helpless to help themselves.

Jesus Raises Lazarus

(John 11)

Jesus loved one special family very much. The family was composed of the sisters Mary and Martha and their brother Lazarus. Jesus had visited in their home and had enjoyed the fellowship and the meals. Mary and Martha, in turn, loved their brother Lazarus dearly.

One day Jesus received the message that Lazarus was very ill. Jesus was ministering to the multitudes and did not hurry to their side. After remaining there two more days, Jesus told his disciples: "Now we will go back to Judea."

When Jesus arrived in Bethany he was told that Lazarus had been in the tomb for four days. When Martha found out that Jesus had arrived, she went to meet him. Martha then said to Jesus: "Lord, if you had been here, my brother would not have died."

Jesus replied: "Your brother will live again." Martha answered: "I know that he will come back to life at the resurrection when all the dead are raised."

Jesus then said to her: "I am the one who brings people from death to life. Everyone who has faith in me will live even if they have died."

Martha then replied: "Lord, I know that you are the Son of God."

Martha then went and told her sister Mary that Jesus had arrived. As soon as Mary saw Jesus she knelt before him and said: "If you had been here my brother would not have died."

Jesus then asked where they had buried the body. When Jesus arrived at the tomb he ordered for the stone to be rolled aside.

Jesus prayed to the Father and then called out in a loud voice: "Lazarus, come out." At that moment Lazarus came out from the tomb. Jesus then ordered for the people to take away the strips of burial cloth from his hands and his feet.

As a result of this miracle, many people put their faith in Jesus.

Note: This story may be helpful in situations in which people have experienced the death of a loved one. Assuring them that Jesus is the one who rose again and has the power to overcome death gives us assurance that we will see our loved ones in heaven if we put our faith in him as our savior.

CONCLUSION

LifeStory Encounters can provide one of the most effective tools for sharing the gospel with oral learners, oral preference people, and literate people throughout the world. In order for this sharing to be effective, however, careful thought and preparation must preceed the actual storying.

In chapter 1, Daniel Sánchez addresses the issue of preparation. This preparation involves reviewing your LifeStory, connecting the dots in your life experiences, clarifying your values, and going from your story to The (Christ's) Story. The practice of engaging in LifeStory encounters begins with sharing your LifeStory with fellow Christians. Listening to the LifeStory of people who need to hear the gospel is often the first step in the storying process. Often people will share stories that center on such themes as joys and achievements, life-shaping influences, sorrows and difficulties, and changes and challenges.

By preparing slice of life stories related to your life, you can be in a position to listen to their story, sharing your story, and sharing The Story. There will be times in which utilizing bridging Bible stories can prepare the person to have a greater understanding of the Story of Jesus. Thinking about these in advance can be greatly beneficial in being prepared to engage in LifeStory Encounters.

In chapter 2, Daniel Sánchez shares a number of inspiring LifeStory experiences that he has had throughout the years. Many of these experiences were totally unexpected, yet having a notion what needed to be done helped him to minister to people and to plant the seeds of the gospel.

In these unplanned encounters, Daniel listened to stories of persons searching for a sense of purpose, experiencing grief, being overwhelmed by a sense of guilt, being deeply troubled, having concern about their children and being on the brink of eternity. He reminds us that people are different one from another. They have a wide variety of experiences some of which are quite unique to them. The important thing is not to try to follow a strict pattern but to be flexible in the way you engage in the LifeStory Encounter and be sensitive to the guidance of the Holy Spirit.

In chapter 3, J.O. Terry shares some of his own personal stories that were foundational in his upbringing and his ministry. He then explains the manner in which personal stories can be powerful in providing bridges for the communication of the gospel story.

In addition to this J.O. gives examples of the way in which stories can elicit a strong and emotional response on the part of the listeners. He then asks the reader: Do you know your own personal story? In order to assist potential storyers, J.O. shares a significant portion of his own LifeStory. He then reminds storyers that they do not live in isolation.

Many people are touched by their stories, therefore, they should be encouraged to write out their own stories and to share them with others. He explains: "Writing is wonderful for preserving the content of our LifeStories, but face to face sharing exchanges not only the content, the facts, but also the emotions we experienced."

In chapter 4, J.O. Terry focuses our attention on the value of utilizing life stories. To begin with, he emphasizes the fact that stories are relational. He then cautions storyers to use culturally appropriate stories that communicate truth but do not create obstacles. He reminds readers that sharing stories requires a deep level of trust, that stories are memorable, that stories are high touch, and that stories are distilled spirit.

He concludes this chapter by encouraging the potential storyers to have confidence in their own story. Cautioning against appropriating someone else's story or depreciating their own story, J.O. Terry emphasizes the value of each individual's story and provides instructions on how storyers can get to know their own story and how they can share it with others.

In Chapter Five J.O. Terry and Daniel Sánchez present a series of

Bible Stories that can be used as bridges to communicate the Gospel Story. Under the themes of Joys and Achievements; Life-Shaping Influences; Sorrows and Difficulties; and Changes and Challenges, the authors have selected Bible stories that connect with the experiences reflected in these themes. The authors have written these stories in a simplified manner to enable the readers to capture the gist of each story and to be in a position to utilize it as a bridge that will prepare people to understand the Story of Christ more clearly and with greater receptivity.

Acknowledging the fact that the stories presented in this chapter are but a few of those found in the Bible, the authors encourage the readers to be open to using additional biblical stories that connect with the experiences of the people to whom they will witness.

As we consider employing the LifeStory Encounter method to reach people with the message of salvation, let us not forget the example Jesus himself left for us. Roy Fairchild reminds us of the fact that we are always amazed by the full attention Jesus gave to the people he encountered:

> He was not in a hurry. Their "interruptions" were his work. He entered people's lives fully, even when he was pressured to do many other things. He refused to respond to a person through a pre-conceived image. He was fully present and acted authentically in each encounter: when he met a woman taken in adultery; confronted a Roman centurion who asked for help; talked about her LifeStory to a woman at a well; went home with a tax extortioner - Zacchaeus; or faced a wine shortage at a joyful wedding. He was fully present where he was. And that is one prerequisite for LifeStory conversations to take place.[28]

Let us "go and do likewise."

ENDNOTES

[1] J.O. Terry, *Basic Bible Storying*, Church Starting Network, 2007. www.churchstarting.net

[2] Daniel R. Sánchez, J.O. Terry, LaNette Thompson, *Bible Storying for Church Planting*, Church Starting Network, 2008, www.churchstarting.net

[3] J.O. Terry, *Bible Storying Handbook: For Short-Term Church Mission Teams and Mission Volunteers*, Church Starting Network, 2008, www.churchstarting.net

[4] J.O. Terry, *Hope Stories From The Bible*, Church Starting Network, 2008, www.churchstarting.net

[5] J.O. Terry, *Guía Para La Narrativa Bíblica* (Spanish Version of Bible Storying Handbook), Church Starting Network, 2008, www.churchstarting.net

[6] Roy W. Fairchild, *LifeStory Conversations* (New York: Evangelism Program of the United Presbyterian Church, USA, 1977).

[7] Ibid., 6.

[8] Fairchild recommends engaging in a life review, searching for meaning, discovering the "Gods" we serve, and linking our story with The story, pp, 14-17.

[9] Ibid., 14.

[10] Ibid., 14.

[11] Ibid., 17.

[12] Ibid., 14.

[13] Ibid. Fairchild suggests: Joys and High Points, Life-Shaping Influences, Troubles and Hurts, and Transitions and Transformations. We have adapted these themes to the purpose of our book.

[14] Ibid., 31.

[15] Dr. Elias Golonka's testimony shared verbally on the occasion described this text. It was my privilege to be a colleague of Dr. Golonka for fifteen years and I

was always inspired to hear his testimony and to observe the manner in which he shared it in a wide variety of settings.

[16] Steve Douglass, Excerpt from *Does Success Really Satisfy?* Unpublished paper, 1.

[17] Ibid, 4, 5.

[18] J.O. Terry, *Basic Bible Storying*, chapter 18.

[19] John Witte in an email to Jon L. Sapp, Friday, July 27, 2001. Subject: The full story on Joseph and Martha Makrer.

[20] "*EE-TAOW!*" video, New Tribes Mission, Sanford, FL.

[21] LaNette Thompson, *Diaradugu Diary*, unpublished diary, International Mission Board, SBC. 1992. p. 4.

[22] Trevor McIlwain, *Building on Firm Foundations*, New Tribes Mission, Sanford: 1987. Vol. 1, p. 34.

[23] *The Village Pump*, Kannok Bannasan (OMF), Bangkok.

[24] John W. Drakeford, *The Awesome Power of the Listening Ear*," Word Books, 1969.

[25] Anne Morrow Lindbergh, *Bring Me a Unicorn: Diaries and Letters of Anne Morrow Lindbergh 1922-1928*, First Harvest/Harcourt, edition 1993.

[26] Benedicte Grima, *Performance of Emotion Among Paxtun Women*, Oxford University Press, Karachi, 1993.,126.

[27] See, J.O. Terry, *Basic Bible Storying*, Church Starting Network, 2007.

[28]. Ibid., 10.

www.ingramcontent.com/pod-product-compliance
Lightning Source LLC
Chambersburg PA
CBHW050829160426
43192CB00010B/1951